Library Learning Information

To renew this item call:

0115 929 3388
or visit
www.ideastore.co.uk

TOWER HAMLETS

Created and managed by Tower Hamlets Council

RUPERT BROOKE

THE POETICAL WORKS

Rupert Brooke

THE POETICAL WORKS

edited by Geoffrey Keynes

ff

FABER & FABER

First published in 1946
by Faber & Faber Ltd
Bloomsbury House
74–77 Great Russell Street
London WC1B 3DA

This edition published in 2014

Printed in England by CPI Group (UK) Ltd, Croydon, CR0 4YY

The right of Geoffrey Keynes to be identified as editor of this work has been
asserted in accordance with Section 77 of the Copyright, Designs and Patents
Act 1988

A CIP record for this book
is available from the British Library

ISBN 978–0–571–31364–8 (HBK)

FSC
www.fsc.org
MIX
Paper from
responsible sources
FSC® C101712

2 4 6 8 10 9 7 5 3 1

Preface

Rupert Brooke published his first volume of poetry in 1911, a slender book containing fifty poems written during the seven years 1905–1911. Poems from his pen were published in various periodicals during the next three years, but no second volume appeared during his lifetime. The five famous War Sonnets were written in the last months of 1914 and were finished at Rugby while he was at home on leave from military service. They were published in December 1914, in the fourth and last part of *New Numbers* with poems by Lascelles Abercrombie, Wilfrid Gibson and John Drinkwater. On April 23, 1915, Brooke died of septicæmia in a French hospital ship in the Aegean, and was buried the same day on the island of Scyros, where a monument has since been built over his grave.

Brooke died in his twenty-eighth year, and so had but little chance to consolidate his growing reputation as a poet; but soon after his death his friend and biographer, Sir Edward Marsh, collected and published a second volume of thirty-two poems covering the years 1911–1914. This began with the War Sonnets and ended with his almost equally well-known poem 'Grantchester', a nostalgic fantasy written around the theme of his Cambridgeshire home while he was travelling in Germany. This second volume appeared in May 1915, and three years later, in 1918, the two books were united inside one cover. A few poems were added in an appendix, and the volume was prefaced by Sir Edward Marsh's sympathetic Memoir. Since that time the public demand for Brooke's poems has never abated, and innumerable reprintings of the original two volumes and of the collection have been made. It is now over thirty years since his death, and it has seemed to the Literary Trustees appointed by his mother in her will that the time has come for a new and enlarged edition of his poems, and it is hoped that it may prove more satisfying to his future readers than further reprints in the old forms.

No re-arrangement of the poems has been made since they first appeared, and since 1918 only one poem has been added. In the present edition the 82 poems of the original two volumes have been increased to 120, and these have been arranged as far as possible in chronological sequence, beginning with the last poems written shortly before his death in 1915, and ending with his earliest pieces written during his school days at Rugby. Among these will be found his two longest poems, 'The Bastille' and 'The Pyramids', composed for the school prize in 1905 and 1904, the later one being successful. These have been printed hitherto only privately or in school magazines. Some of the other pieces also appeared in similar publications or have remained in manuscript.

As editor of this collection and originator of the project I have no wish to make any exaggerated claim as to the importance of the poems that have been added. It may be frankly admitted that they are but *juvenilia,* which the author might never have himself included in any collection had he lived to write more – and better – poetry. But when a poet has passed his third decade of posthumous fame and has come to be accepted as a national possession, his early efforts acquire an interest for the evidence they afford of the influences at work during formative years, even though their literary merit be not great. Although 38 poems have now been added to the *corpus* of Brooke's work, many others still remain uncollected, having been rejected at the discretion of the Trustees as unworthy of inclusion now or at any future date. The names of my co-Trustees, Mr Walter de la Mare, the Provost of King's College, and Mr Dudley Ward, who also had the views of Mr Wilfrid Gibson and the late Dr Francis Cornford, will be proof enough that this censorship has not been exercised without due regard to the reputation of the poet. All of us were his friends and most of us can recall the circumstances in which individual poems were written. Many of the early pieces carry my own memories back to our school days, when my admiration for their merits was no doubt less influenced than now by any critical reservations. Brooke was a precocious and voracious reader of poetry and minor verse. Before he was eighteen he had absorbed the great Victorians, and affected to think Tennyson old-fashioned, though he still admitted to an admiration for Browning. Of the lesser poets he often quoted Housman with approval. At eighteen his enthusiasms were the natural tastes of his age – Rossetti, Swinburne, Dowson, Wilde, whose contributions may be discerned in some of the pieces now printed. Swinburne in particular he would learn by heart, and he delighted to declaim long passages during our country walks round Rugby. The first book he gave me, early in 1906, was a translation of Baudelaire's poems, and this was an influence that lasted through the period in which the poems in his first volume were written. It amused him to assume some of the affectations of the 'nineties, and on the flyleaf of the Baudelaire volume he wrote a quotation from Wilde, 'One should always be a little improbable.' At the same time he was beginning to read more of Donne and the Elizabethans, particularly Marlowe and Webster. This interest culminated in his dissertation on 'Webster and the Elizabethan Drama', written in 1911–1912 for a Fellowship at King's College, Cambridge.

During his later years his appetite for contemporary verse, especially that of W. B. Yeats, remained unabated, but his activities centred more in the Fabian brand of Socialism which he had adopted as an undergraduate at Cambridge, and literary influences grew less. At the same time, as he matured, his emotional life coloured his poetry with more genuine feeling than before. Nearly every one of his later poems, other than fantasies such as 'The Funeral of Youth', was inspired by his own experiences, though few of his friends knew of the heights and the depths of the emotional crises through which he passed.

In recent years, with the changed fashion in the writing of verse, some of the younger critics have challenged the popular favour accorded so lavishly and continuously to Brooke's poetry, and they have tried to demolish his literary reputation, sometimes with words of scorn. The circumstances of his early death together with the appeal of the War Sonnets may have given an undue impetus in 1915 to his growing fame; but it seems improbable that popular opinion will now be reversed. Brooke was no callow youth when he died, and the notes that he sounded in his later poems were those of a sincere and deep feeling,

The text of this collection of Brooke's poems has been carefully revised, and a number of errors that had crept in through numerous reprintings have been eliminated. The volume of 1911 and the four parts of *New Numbers* have been taken as the final authority for all the poems that they contain, since these were read in proof by Brooke himself. The poems that were added in the volume of 1915, edited by Sir Edward Marsh, were partly printed from manuscripts. Comparison with these original sources shews that the editor allowed himself sometimes to introduce minor changes when the rough drafts at his disposal seemed to contain imperfections which the author would himself have wished to improve. These changes have usually not been disturbed, no one being better able to interpret Brooke's mind than was his first editor. The additional poems have been printed from original sources, many of them being from manuscripts in my possession.

September 1946

In this second edition some minor corrections have been made, also changes in 'The Night Journey' (p. 35) authorized by a fair copy of the poem now in my keeping. Similarly a dropped word has been restored to the fourth line of 'Evening' (p. 161) derived from a fair copy recently acquired by King's College, Cambridge. The only substantive addition to the canon is a collection of 'Fragments' written during the voyage to Gallipoli in April 1915 shortly before Brooke's death. These were first printed by Sir Edward Marsh in the Memoir prefixed to the *Collected Poems* in 1918.

September 1969

A text of 'The Bastille' corrected by the author has been incorporated in the 1974 reprint.

GEOFFREY KEYNES

Contents

THE POETICAL WORKS

Fragment

I strayed about the deck, an hour, to-night
Under a cloudy moonless sky; and peeped
In at the windows, watched my friends at table,
Or playing cards, or standing in the doorway,
Or coming out into the darkness. Still
No one could see me.

                   I would have thought of them
– Heedless, within a week of battle – in pity,
Pride in their strength and in the weight and firmness
And link'd beauty of bodies, and pity that
This gay machine of splendour I'd soon be broken,
Thought little of, pashed, scattered. . . .

                     Only, always,
I could but see them – against the lamplight – pass
Like coloured shadows, thinner than filmy glass,
Slight bubbles, fainter than the wave's faint light,
That broke to phosphorus out in the night,
Perishing things and strange ghosts – soon to die
To other ghosts – this one, or that, or I.

April 1915

The Dance

A SONG

As the Wind, and as the Wind,
  In a corner of the way,
Goes skipping, stands twirling,
Invisibly, comes whirling,
Bows before, and skips behind,
  In a grave, an endless play –

So my Heart, and so my Heart,
  Following where your feet have gone,
Stirs dust of old dreams there;
He turns a toe; he gleams there,
Treading you a dance apart.
  But you see not. You pass on.

April 1915

1914

I

Peace

Now, God be thanked Who has matched us with His hour,
   And caught our youth, and wakened us from sleeping,
With hand made sure, clear eye, and sharpened power,
   To turn, as swimmers into cleanness leaping,
Glad from a world grown old and cold and weary,
   Leave the sick hearts that honour could not move,
And half-men, and their dirty songs and dreary,
   And all the little emptiness of love!

Oh! we, who have known shame, we have found release there,
   Where there's no ill, no grief, but sleep has mending,
      Naught broken save this body, lost but breath;
Nothing to shake the laughing heart's long peace there
   But only agony, and that has ending;
      And the worst friend and enemy is but Death.

II

Safety

Dear! of all happy in the hour, most blest
   He who has found our hid security,
Assured in the dark tides of the world that rest,
   And heard our word, 'Who is so safe as we?'
We have found safety with all things undying,
   The winds, and morning, tears of men and mirth,
The deep night, and birds singing, and clouds flying,
   And sleep, and freedom, and the autumnal earth.

We have built a house that is not for Time's throwing.
   We have gained a peace unshaken by pain for ever.
War knows no power. Safe shall be my going,
   Secretly armed against all death's endeavour;
Safe though all safety's lost; safe where men fall;
And if these poor limbs die, safest of all.

III

The Dead

Blow out, you bugles, over the rich Dead!
   There's none of these so lonely and poor of old,
   But, dying, has made us rarer gifts than gold.
These laid the world away; poured out the red
Sweet wine of youth; gave up the years to be
   Of work and joy, and that unhoped serene,
   That men call age; and those who would have been,
Their sons, they gave, their immortality.

Blow, bugles, blow! They brought us, for our dearth,
   Holiness, lacked so long, and Love, and Pain.
Honour has come back, as a king, to earth,
   And paid his subjects with a royal wage;
And Nobleness walks in our ways again;
   And we have come into our heritage.

IV

The Dead

These hearts were woven of human joys and cares,
    Washed marvellously with sorrow, swift to mirth.
The years had given them kindness. Dawn was theirs,
    And sunset, and the colours of the earth.
These had seen movement, and heard music; known
    Slumber and waking; loved; gone proudly friended;
Felt the quick stir of wonder; sat alone;
    Touched flowers and furs and cheeks. All this is ended.

There are waters blown by changing winds to laughter
And lit by the rich skies, all day. And after,
    Frost, with a gesture, stays the waves that dance
And wandering loveliness. He leaves a white
    Unbroken glory, a gathered radiance,
A width, a shining peace, under the night.

V

The Soldier

If I should die, think only this of me:
    That there's some corner of a foreign field
That is for ever England. There shall be
    In that rich earth a richer dust concealed;
A dust whom England bore, shaped, made aware,
    Gave, once, her flowers to love, her ways to roam,
A body of England's, breathing English air,
    Washed by the rivers, blest by suns of home.

And think, this heart, all evil shed away,
    A pulse in the eternal mind, no less
        Gives somewhere back the thoughts by England given;
Her sights and sounds; dreams happy as her day;
    And laughter, learnt of friends; and gentleness,
        In hearts at peace, under an English heaven.

November–December 1914

The Treasure

When colour goes home into the eyes,
    And lights that shine are shut again,
With dancing girls and sweet birds' cries
    Behind the gateways of the brain;
And that no-place which gave them birth, shall close
The rainbow and the rose: –

Still may Time hold some golden space
    Where I'll unpack that scented store
Of song and flower and sky and face,
    And count, and touch, and turn them o'er,
Musing upon them; as a mother, who
Has watched her children all the rich day through,
Sits, quiet-handed, in the fading light,
When children sleep, ere night.

August 1914

Tiare Tahiti

Mamua, when our laughter ends,
And hearts and bodies, brown as white,
Are dust about the doors of friends,
Or scent a-blowing down the night,
Then, oh! then, the wise agree,
Comes our immortality.
Mamua, there waits a land
Hard for us to understand.
Out of time, beyond the sun,
All are one in Paradise,
You and Pupure[1] are one,
And Taü, and the ungainly wise.
There the Eternals are, and there
The Good, the Lovely, and the True,
And Types, whose earthly copies were
The foolish broken things we knew;
There is the face, whose ghosts we are;
The real, the never-setting Star;
And the Flower, of which we love
Faint and fading shadows here;
Never a tear, but only Grief;
Dance, but not the limbs that move;
Songs in Song shall disappear;
Instead of lovers, Love shall be;
For hearts, Immutability;
And there, on the Ideal Reef,
Thunders the Everlasting Sea!

---

[1] Tahitian for 'fair', the name given to himself.

And my laughter, and my pain,
Shall home to the Eternal Brain.
And all lovely things, they say,
Meet in Loveliness again;
Miri's laugh, Teïpo's feet,
And the hands of Matua,
Stars and sunlight there shall meet,
Coral's hues and rainbows there,
And Teüra's braided hair;
And with the starred *tiare's* white,
And white birds in the dark ravine,
And *flamboyants* ablaze at night,
And jewels, and evening's after-green,
And dawns of pearl and gold and red,
Mamua, your lovelier head!
And there'll no more be one who dreams
Under the ferns, of crumbling stuff,
Eyes of illusion, mouth that seems,
All time-entangled human love.
And you'll no longer swing and sway
Divinely down the scented shade,
Where feet to Ambulation fade,
And moons are lost in endless Day.
How shall we wind these wreaths of ours,
Where there are neither heads nor flowers?
Oh, Heaven's Heaven! – but we'll be
    missing
The palms, and sunlight, and the south;
And there's an end, I think, of kissing,
When our mouths are one with Mouth . . .

Taü here, Mamua,
Crown the hair, and come away!
Hear the calling of the moon,
And the whispering scents that stray
About the idle warm lagoon.
Hasten, hand in human hand,
Down the dark, the flowered way,
Along the whiteness of the sand,
And in the water's soft caress,
Wash the mind of foolishness,
Mamua, until the day.
Spend the glittering moonlight there
Pursuing down the soundless deep
Limbs that gleam and shadowy hair,
Or floating lazy, half-asleep.
Dive and double and follow after,
Snare in flowers, and kiss, and call,
With lips that fade, and human laughter,
And faces individual,
Well this side of Paradise! . . .
There's little comfort in the wise.

Papeete, February 1914

Retrospect

In your arms was still delight,
Quiet as a street at night;
And thoughts of you, I do remember,
Were green leaves in a darkened chamber,
Were dark clouds in a moonless sky.
Love, in you, went passing by,
Penetrative, remote, and rare,
Like a bird in the wide air,
And, as the bird, it left no trace
In the heaven of your face.

In your stupidity I found
The sweet hush after a sweet sound.
All about you was the light
That dims the greying end of night;
Desire was the unrisen sun,
Joy the day not yet begun,
With tree whispering to tree,
Without wind, quietly.
Wisdom slept within your hair,
And Long-Suffering was there,
And, in the flowing of your dress,
Undiscerning Tenderness.
And when you thought, it seemed to me,
Infinitely, and like a sea,
About the slight world you had known
Your vast unconsciousness was thrown. . . .

O haven without wave or tide!
Silence, in which all songs have died!

Holy book, where hearts are still!
And home at length under the hill!
O mother-quiet, breasts of peace,
Where love itself would faint and cease!
O infinite deep I never knew,
I would come back, come back to you,
Find you, as a pool unstirred,
Kneel down by you, and never a word,
Lay my head, and nothing said,
In your hands, ungarlanded;
And a long watch you would keep;
And I should sleep, and I should sleep!

Mataiea, January 1914

The Great Lover

I have been so great a lover: filled my days
So proudly with the splendour of Love's praise,
The pain, the calm, and the astonishment,
Desire illimitable, and still content,
And all dear names men use, to cheat despair,
For the perplexed and viewless streams that bear
Our hearts at random down the dark of life.
Now, ere the unthinking silence on that strife
Steals down, I would cheat drowsy Death so far,
My night shall be remembered for a star
That outshone all the suns of all men's days.
Shall I not crown them with immortal praise
Whom I have loved, who have given me, dared with me
High secrets, and in darkness knelt to see
The inenarrable godhead of delight?
Love is a flame: – we have beaconed the world's night.
A city: – and we have built it, these and I.
An emperor: – we have taught the world to die.
So, for their sakes I loved, ere I go hence,
And the high cause of Love's magnificence,
And to keep loyalties young, I'll write those names
Golden for ever, eagles, crying flames,
And set them as a banner, that men may know,
To dare the generations, burn, and blow
Out on the wind of Time, shining and streaming. . . .
These I have loved:

        White plates and cups, clean-gleaming,
Ringed with blue lines; and feathery, faery dust;
Wet roofs, beneath the lamp-light; the strong crust
Of friendly bread; and many-tasting food;

Rainbows; and the blue bitter smoke of wood;
And radiant raindrops couching in cool flowers;
And flowers themselves, that sway through sunny hours,
Dreaming of moths that drink them under the moon;
Then, the cool kindliness of sheets, that soon
Smooth away trouble; and the rough male kiss
Of blankets; grainy wood; live hair that is
Shining and free; blue-massing clouds; the keen
Unpassioned beauty of a great machine;
The benison of hot water; furs to touch;
The good smell of old clothes; and others such –
The comfortable smell of friendly fingers,
Hair's fragrance, and the musty reek that lingers
About dead leaves and last year's ferns. . . .

                                        Dear names,
And thousand other throng to me! Royal flames;
Sweet water's dimpling laugh from tap or spring;
Holes in the ground; and voices that do sing;
Voices in laughter, too; and body's pain,
Soon turned to peace; and the deep-panting train;
Firm sands; the little dulling edge of foam
That browns and dwindles as the wave goes home;
And washen stones, gay for an hour; the cold
Graveness of iron; moist black earthen mould;
Sleep; and high places; footprints in the dew;
And oaks; and brown horse-chestnuts, glossy-new;
And new-peeled sticks; and shining pools on grass; –
All these have been my loves. And these shall pass,
Whatever passes not, in the great hour,
Nor all my passion, all my prayers, have power

To hold them with me through the gate of Death.
They'll play deserter, turn with the traitor breath,
Break the high bond we made, and sell Love's trust
And sacramented covenant to the dust.
———Oh, never a doubt but, somewhere, I shall wake,
And give what's left of love again, and make
New friends, now strangers. . . .
                                   But the best I've known
Stays here, and changes, breaks, grows old, is blown
About the winds of the world, and fades from brains
Of living men, and dies.
                         Nothing remains.

O dear my loves, O faithless, once again
This one last gift I give: that after men
Shall know, and later lovers, far-removed,
Praise you, 'All these were lovely'; say, 'He loved.'

Mataiea, 1914

Hauntings

In the grey tumult of these after-years
   Oft silence falls; the incessant wranglers part;
And less-than-echoes of remembered tears
   Hush all the loud confusion of the heart;
And a shade, through the toss'd ranks of mirth and crying,
   Hungers, and pains, and each dull passionate mood, –
Quite lost, and all but all forgot, undying,
   Comes back the ecstasy of your quietude.

So a poor ghost, beside his misty streams,
Is haunted by strange doubts, evasive dreams,
   Hints of a pre-Lethean life, of men,
Stars, rocks, and flesh, things unintelligible,
   And light on waving grass, he knows not when,
And feet that ran, but where, he cannot tell.

The Pacific, 1914

Fafaïa

Stars that seem so close and bright,
Watched by lovers through the night,
Swim in emptiness, men say,
Many a mile and year away.

And yonder star that burns so white,
May have died to dust and night
Ten, maybe, or fifteen year,
Before it shines upon my dear.

Oh! often among men below,
Heart cries out to heart, I know,
And one is dust a many years,
Child, before the other hears.

Heart from heart is all as far,
Fafaïa, as star from star.

Saanapu, November 1913

Heaven

Fish (fly-replete, in depth of June,
Dawdling away their wat'ry noon)
Ponder deep wisdom, dark or clear,
Each secret fishy hope or fear.
Fish say, they have their Stream and Pond;
But is there anything Beyond?
This life cannot be All, they swear,
For how unpleasant, if it were!
One may not doubt that, somehow, Good
Shall come of Water and of Mud;
And, sure, the reverent eye must see
A Purpose in Liquidity.
We darkly know, by Faith we cry,
The future is not Wholly Dry.
Mud unto mud! – Death eddies near –
Not here the appointed End, not here!
But somewhere, beyond Space and Time,
Is wetter water, slimier slime!
And there (they trust) there swimmeth One
Who swam ere rivers were begun,
Immense, of fishy form and mind,
Squamous, omnipotent, and kind;
And under that Almighty Fin,
The littlest fish may enter in.
Oh! never fly conceals a hook,
Fish say, in the Eternal Brook,
But more than mundane weeds are there,
And mud, celestially fair;
Fat caterpillars drift around,
And Paradisal grubs are found;

Unfading moths, immortal flies,
And the worm that never dies.
And in that Heaven of all their wish,
There shall be no more land, say fish.

1913

Waikiki

Warm perfumes like a breath from vine and tree
   Drift down the darkness. Plangent, hidden from eyes,
   Somewhere an *eukaleli* thrills and cries
And stabs with pain the night's brown savagery;
And dark scents whisper; and dim waves creep to me,
   Gleam like a woman's hair, stretch out, and rise;
   And new stars burn into the ancient skies,
Over the murmurous soft Hawaian sea.

And I recall, lose, grasp, forget again,
   And still remember, a tale I have heard, or known,
An empty tale, of idleness and pain,
   Of two that loved – or did not love – and one
Whose perplexed heart did evil, foolishly,
A long while since, and by some other sea.

Waikiki, 1913

One Day

To-day I have been happy. All the day
  I held the memory of you, and wove
Its laughter with the dancing light o' the spray,
  And sowed the sky with tiny clouds of love,
And sent you following the white waves of sea,
    And crowned your head with fancies, nothing
       worth,
Stray buds from that old dust of misery,
  Being glad with a new foolish quiet mirth.

So lightly I played with those dark memories,
Just as a child, beneath the summer skies,
  Plays hour by hour with a strange shining stone,
For which (he knows not) towns were fire of old,
  And love has been betrayed, and murder done,
And great kings turned to a little bitter mould.

The Pacific, October 1913

A Memory

From a sonnet-sequence

Somewhile before the dawn I rose, and stept
   Softly along the dim way to your room,
   And found you sleeping in the quiet gloom,
And holiness about you as you slept.
I knelt there; till your waking fingers crept
   About my head, and held it. I had rest
   Unhoped this side of Heaven, beneath your breast.
I knelt a long time, still; nor even wept.

It was great wrong you did me; and for gain
Of that poor moment's kindliness, and ease,
And sleepy mother-comfort!
                Child, you know
How easily love leaps out to dreams like these,
Who has seen them true. And love that's wakened so
Takes all too long to lay asleep again.

Waikiki, October 1913

Sonnet

Suggested by some of the Proceedings of the Society for Psychical Research

Not with vain tears, when we're beyond the sun,
  We'll beat on the substantial doors, nor tread
  Those dusty high-roads of the aimless dead
Plaintive for Earth; but rather turn and run
Down some close-covered by-way of the air,
  Some low sweet alley between wind and wind,
  Stoop under faint gleams, thread the shadows, find
Some whispering ghost-forgotten nook, and there
Spend in pure converse our eternal day;
  Think each in each, immediately wise;
Learn all we lacked before; hear, know, and say
  What this tumultuous body now denies;
And feel, who have laid our groping hands away;
  And see, no longer blinded by our eyes.

1913

[26]

Clouds

Down the blue night the unending columns press
  In noiseless tumult, break and wave and flow,
  Now tread the far South, or lift rounds of snow
Up to the white moon's hidden loveliness.
Some pause in their grave wandering comradeless,
  And turn with profound gesture vague and slow,
  As who would pray good for the world, but know
Their benediction empty as they bless.

They say that the Dead die not, but remain
  Near to the rich heirs of their grief and mirth.
    I think they ride the calm mid-heaven, as these,
In wise majestic melancholy train,
  And watch the moon, and the still-raging seas,
  And men, coming and going on the earth.

The Pacific, October 1913

[27]

There's Wisdom in Women

'Oh love is fair, and love is rare;' my dear one she said,
'But love goes lightly over.' I bowed her foolish head,
And kissed her hair and laughed at her. Such a child was she;
So new to love, so true to love, and she spoke so bitterly.

But there's wisdom in women, of more than they have known,
And thoughts go blowing through them, are wiser than their own,
Or how should my dear one, being ignorant and young,
Have cried on love so bitterly, with so true a tongue?

June 1913

Doubts

When she sleeps, her soul, I know,
Goes a wanderer on the air,
Wings where I may never go,
Leaves her lying, still and fair,
Waiting, empty, laid aside,
Like a dress upon a chair. . . .
This I know, and yet I know
Doubts that will not be denied.

For if the soul be not in place,
What has laid trouble in her face?
And, sits there nothing ware and wise
Behind the curtains of her eyes,
What is it, in the self's eclipse,
Shadows, soft and passingly,
About the corners of her lips,
The smile that is essential she?

And if the spirit be not there,
Why is fragrance in the hair?

1913

He wonders whether to Praise or
to Blame Her

I have peace to weigh your worth, now all is over,
   But if to praise or blame you, cannot say.
For, who decries the loved, decries the lover;
   Yet what man lauds the thing he's thrown away?

Be you, in truth, this dull, slight, cloudy naught,
   The more fool I, so great a fool to adore;
But if you're that high goddess once I thought,
   The more your godhead is, I lose the more.

Dear fool, pity the fool who thought you clever!
   Dear wisdom, do not mock the fool that missed you!
Most fair, – the blind has lost your face for ever!
   Most foul, – how could I see you while I kissed you?

So . . . the poor love of fools and blind I've proved you,
For, foul or lovely, 'twas a fool that loved you.

1913

Mutability

They say there's a high windless world and strange,
  Out of the wash of days and temporal tide,
  Where Faith and Good, Wisdom and Truth abide,
Æterna corpora, subject to no change.

There the sure suns of these pale shadows move;
  There stand the immortal ensigns of our war;
  Our melting flesh fixed Beauty there, a star,
And perishing hearts, imperishable Love. . . .

Dear, we know only that we sigh, kiss, smile;
  Each kiss lasts but the kissing; and grief goes over;
  Love has no habitation but the heart.
Poor straws! on the dark flood we catch awhile,
  Cling, and are borne into the night apart.
  The laugh dies with the lips, 'Love' with the lover.

South Kensington – Makaweli, 1913

The Funeral of Youth: Threnody

The day that *Youth* had died,
There came to his grave-side,
In decent mourning, from the county's ends,
Those scatter'd friends
Who had lived the boon companions of his prime,
And laughed with him and sung with him and wasted,
In feast and wine and many-crown'd carouse,
The days and nights and dawnings of the time
When *Youth* kept open house,
Nor left untasted
Aught of his high emprise and ventures dear,
No quest of his unshar'd –
All these, with loitering feet and sad head bar'd,
Followed their old friend's bier.
Folly went first,
With muffled bells and coxcomb still revers'd;
And after trod the bearers, hat in hand –
Laughter, most hoarse, and Captain *Pride* with tanned
And martial face all grim, and fussy *Joy*,
Who had to catch a train, and *Lust*, poor snivelling boy;
These bore the dear departed.
Behind them, broken-hearted,
Came *Grief*, so noisy a widow, that all said,
'Had he but wed
Her elder sister *Sorrow*, in her stead!'
And by her, trying to soothe her all the time,
The fatherless children, *Colour*, *Tune*, and *Rhyme*,
(The sweet lad *Rhyme*), ran all-uncomprehending.
Then, at the way's sad ending,
Round the raw grave they stay'd. Old *Wisdom* read

In mumbling tone the Service for the Dead.
There stood *Romance*,
The furrowing tears had mark'd her rougèd cheek;
Poor old *Conceit*, his wonder unassaug'd;
Dead *Innocency's* daughter, *Ignorance*;
And shabby, ill-dress'd *Generosity*;
And *Argument*, too full of woe to speak;
Passion, grown portly, something middle-ag'd;
And *Friendship* – not a minute older, she;
Impatience, ever taking out his watch;
Faith, who was deaf, and had to lean, to catch
Old *Wisdom's* endless drone.
Beauty was there,
Pale in her black; dry-eyed; she stood alone.
Poor maz'd *Imagination*; *Fancy* wild;
Ardour, the sunlight on his greying hair;
Contentment, who had known *Youth* as a child
And never seen him since. And *Spring* came too,
Dancing over the tombs, and brought him flowers –
She did not stay for long.
And *Truth*, and *Grace*, and all the merry crew,
The laughing *Winds* and *Rivers*, and lithe *Hours*;
And *Hope*, the dewy-eyed; and sorrowing *Song*; –
Yes, with much woe and mourning general,
At dead *Youth's* funeral,
Even these were met once more together, all,
Who erst the fair and living *Youth* did know;
All, except only *Love*. *Love* had died long ago.

1913

The Way that Lovers Use

The way that lovers use is this;
    They bow, catch hands, with never a word,
And their lips meet, and they do kiss,
    – So I have heard.

They queerly find some healing so,
    And strange attainment in the touch;
There is a secret lovers know,
    – I have read as much.

And theirs no longer joy nor smart,
    Changing or ending, night or day;
But mouth to mouth, and heart on heart,
    – So lovers say.

1913

The Night Journey

Hands and lit faces eddy to a line;
    The dazed last minutes click; the clamour dies.
Beyond the great-swung arc o' the roof, divine,
    Night, smoky-scarv'd, with thousand coloured eyes

Glares the imperious mystery of the way.
    Thirsty for dark, you feel the long-limbed train
Throb, stretch, thrill motion, slide, pull out and sway,
    Strain for the far, pause, draw to strength again. . . .

– As a man, caught by some great hour, will rise,
    Slow-limbed, to meet the light or find his love;
And, breathing long, with staring sightless eyes,
    Hands out, head back, agape and silent, move

Sure as a flood, smooth as a vast wind blowing;
    And, gathering power and godhead as he goes,
Unstumbling, unreluctant, strong, unknowing,
    Borne by a will not his, that lifts, that grows,

Sweep into darkness, triumphing to his goal,
    Out of the fire, out of the little room! . . .
– There is an end appointed, O my soul!
    Crimson and green the signals burn. The gloom

Is hung with steam's fantastic livid streamers.
    Lost into God, as lights in light, we fly,
Grown one with will, end-drunken huddled dreamers.
    The white lights roar; the sounds of the world die;

And lips and laughter are forgotten things.
  Speed sharpens; grows. Into the night, and on,
The strength and splendour of our purpose swings.
  The lamps fade; and the stars. We are alone.

1913

Home

I came back late and tired last night
   Into my little room,
To the long chair and the firelight
   And comfortable gloom.

But as I entered softly in
   I saw a woman there,
The line of neck and cheek and chin,
   The darkness of her hair,
The form of one I did not know
   Sitting in my chair.

I stood a moment fierce and still,
   Watching her neck and hair.
I made a step to her; and saw
   That there was no one there.

It was some trick of the firelight
   That made me see her there.
It was a chance of shade and light
   And the cushion in the chair.

Oh, all you happy over the earth,
   That night, how could I sleep?
I lay and watched the lonely gloom;
   And watched the moonlight creep
From wall to basin, round the room.
   All night I could not sleep.

1913

The Chilterns

Your hands, my dear, adorable,
   Your lips of tenderness
– Oh, I've loved you faithfully and well,
   Three years, or a bit less.
   It wasn't a success.

Thank God, that's done! and I'll take the road,
   Quit of my youth and you,
The Roman road to Wendover
   By Tring and Lilley Hoo,
   As a free man may do.

For youth goes over, the joys that fly,
   The tears that follow fast;
And the dirtiest things we do must lie
   Forgotten at the last;
   Even Love goes past.

What's left behind I shall not find,
   The splendour and the pain;
The splash of sun, the shouting wind,
   And the brave sting of rain,
   I may not meet again.

But the years, that take the best away,
   Give something in the end;
And a better friend than love have they,
   For none to mar or mend,
   That have themselves to friend.

I shall desire and I shall find
  The best of my desires;
The autumn road, the mellow wind
  That soothes the darkening shires,
  And laughter, and inn-fires.

White mist about the black hedgerows,
  The slumbering Midland plain,
The silence where the clover grows,
  And the dead leaves in the lane,
  Certainly, these remain.

And I shall find some girl perhaps,
  And a better one than you,
With eyes as wise, but kindlier,
  And lips as soft, but true.
  And I daresay she will do.

1913

Love

Love is a breach in the walls, a broken gate,
  Where that comes in that shall not go again;
Love sells the proud heart's citadel to Fate.
  They have known shame, who love unloved. Even then
When two mouths, thirsty each for each, find slaking,
  And agony's forgot, and hushed the crying
Of credulous hearts, in heaven – such are but taking
  Their own poor dreams within their arms, and lying
Each in his lonely night, each with a ghost.
  Some share that night. But they know, love grows colder,
Grows false and dull, that was sweet lies at most.
  Astonishment is no more in hand or shoulder,
But darkens, and dies out from kiss to kiss.
All this is love; and all love is but this.

1913

It's not going to Happen Again

I have known the most dear that is granted us here,
    More supreme than the gods know above,
Like a star I was hurled through the sweet of the world,
    And the height and the light of it, Love.
I have risen to the uttermost Heaven of Joy,
    I have sunk to the sheer Hell of Pain –
But – it's not going to happen again, my boy,
    It's not going to happen again.

It's the very first word that poor Juliet heard
    From her Romeo over the Styx;
And the Roman will tell Cleopatra in hell
    When she starts the immortal old tricks;
What Paris was tellin' for good-bye to Helen
    When he bundled her into the train –
Oh, it's not going to happen again, old girl,
    It's not going to happen again.

Château Lake Louise
Canada 1913

[41]

The Young Man in April

In the queer light, in twilight,
   In April of the year,
I meet a thousand women,
   But I never meet my Dear.
Yet each of them has something,
   A turn of neck or knee,
A line of breast or shoulder,
   That brings my Dear to me.

One has a way of swaying,
   I'd swear to anywhere;
One has a laugh, and one a hat,
   And one a trick of hair;
– Oh, glints and hints and gestures,
   When shall I find complete
The Dear that's walking somewhere,
   The Dear I've yet to meet?

May 1913

The Busy Heart

Now that we've done our best and worst, and parted,
  I would fill my mind with thoughts that will not rend.
(O heart, I do not dare go empty-hearted)
  I'll think of Love in books, Love without end;
Women with child, content; and old men sleeping;
  And wet strong ploughlands, scarred for certain grain;
And babes that weep, and so forget their weeping;
  And the young heavens, forgetful after rain;
And evening hush, broken by homing wings;
  And Song's nobility, and Wisdom holy,
That live, we dead. I would think of a thousand things,
  Lovely and durable, and taste them slowly,
One after one, like tasting a sweet food.
I have need to busy my heart with quietude.

1913

Song

The way of Love was thus.
He was born, one winter morn,
With hands delicious.
And it was well with us.

Love came our quiet way,
Lit pride in us, and died in us,
All in a winter's day.
There is no more to say.

1913

The True Beatitude

(BOUTS-RIMÉS)

They say, when the Great Prompter's hand shall ring
  Down the last curtain upon earth and sea,
  All the Good Mimes will have eternity
To praise their Author, worship love and sing;

Or to the walls of Heaven wandering
  Look down on those damned for a fretful d——,
  Mock them (all theologians agree
On this reward for virtue), laugh, and fling

New sulphur on the sin-incarnadined . . .
  Ah, Love! still temporal, and still atmospheric,
    Teleologically unperturbed,
We share a peace by no divine divined,
  An earthly garden hidden from any cleric,
    Untrodden of God, by no Eternal curbed.

1913

[45]

Unfortunate

Heart, you are restless as a paper scrap
   That's tossed down dusty pavements by the wind;
   Saying, 'She is most wise, patient and kind.
Between the small hands folded in her lap
Surely a shamed head may bow down at length,
   And find forgiveness where the shadows stir
About her lips, and wisdom in her strength,
   Peace in her peace. Come to her, come to her!' . . .

She will not care. She'll smile to see me come,
   So that I think all Heaven in flower to fold me.
   She'll give me all I ask, kiss me and hold me,
     And open wide upon that holy air
The gates of peace, and take my tiredness home,
     Kinder than God. But, heart, she will not care.

1912

Mary and Gabriel

Young Mary, loitering once her garden way,
Felt a warm splendour grow in the April day,
As wine that blushes water through. And soon,
Out of the gold air of the afternoon,
One knelt before her: hair he had, or fire,
Bound back above his ears with golden wire,
Baring the eager marble of his face.
Not man's nor woman's was the immortal grace
Rounding the limbs beneath that robe of white,
And lighting the proud eyes with changeless light,
Incurious. Calm as his wings, and fair,
That presence filled the garden.
                                        She stood there,
Saying, 'What would you, Sir?'
                                        He told his word,
'Blessed art thou of women!' Half she heard,
Hands folded and face bowed, half long had known,
The message of that clear and holy tone,
That fluttered hot sweet sobs about her heart;
Such serene tidings moved such human smart.
Her breath came quick as little flakes of snow.
Her hands crept up her breast. She did but know
It was not hers. She felt a trembling stir
Within her body, a will too strong for her
That held and filled and mastered all. With eyes
Closed, and a thousand soft short broken sighs,
She gave submission; fearful, meek, and glad. . . .

She wished to speak. Under her breasts she had
Such multitudinous burnings, to and fro,
And throbs not understood; she did not know

If they were hurt or joy for her; but only
That she was grown strange to herself, half lonely,
All wonderful, filled full of pains to come
And thoughts she dare not think, swift thoughts and dumb,
Human, and quaint, her own, yet very far,
Divine, dear, terrible, familiar . . .
Her heart was faint for telling; to relate
Her limbs' sweet treachery, her strange high estate,
Over and over, whispering, half revealing,
Weeping; and so find kindness to her healing.
'Twixt tears and laughter, panic hurrying her,
She raised her eyes to that fair messenger.
He knelt unmoved, immortal; with his eyes
Gazing beyond her, calm to the calm skies;
Radiant, untroubled in his wisdom, kind.
His sheaf of lilies stirred not in the wind.
How should she, pitiful with mortality,
Try the wide peace of that felicity
With ripples of her perplexed shaken heart,
And hints of human ecstasy, human smart,
And whispers of the lonely weight she bore,
And how her womb within was hers no more
And at length hers?

           Being tired, she bowed her head;
And said, 'So be it!'

           The great wings were spread,
Showering glory on the fields, and fire.
The whole air, singing, bore him up, and higher,

Unswerving, unreluctant. Soon he shone
A gold speck in the gold skies; then was gone.

The air was colder, and grey. She stood alone.

Autumn 1912

Song

All suddenly the wind comes soft,
    And Spring is here again;
And the hawthorn quickens with buds of green,
    And my heart with buds of pain.

My heart all Winter lay so numb,
    The earth so dead and frore,
That I never thought the Spring would come,
    Or my heart wake any more.

But Winter's broken and earth has woken,
    And the small birds cry again;
And the hawthorn hedge puts forth its buds,
    And my heart puts forth its pain.

1912

Beauty and Beauty

When Beauty and Beauty meet
   All naked, fair to fair,
The earth is crying-sweet,
   And scattering-bright the air,
Eddying, dizzying, closing round,
   With soft and drunken laughter;
Veiling all that may befall
   After – after –

Where Beauty and Beauty met,
   Earth's still a-tremble there,
And the winds are scented yet,
   And memory-soft the air,
Bosoming, folding glints of light,
   And shreds of shadowy laughter;
Not the tears that fill the years
   After – after –

1912

The Old Vicarage, Grantchester

Café des Westens, Berlin, May 1912

Just now the lilac is in bloom,
All before my little room;
And in my flower-beds, I think,
Smile the carnation and the pink;
And down the borders, well I know,
The poppy and the pansy blow . . .
Oh! there the chestnuts, summer through,
Beside the river make for you
A tunnel of green gloom, and sleep
Deeply above; and green and deep
The stream mysterious glides beneath,
Green as a dream and deep as death.
– Oh, damn! I know it! and I know
How the May fields all golden show,
And when the day is young and sweet,
Gild gloriously the bare feet
That run to bathe . . .
                              Du lieber Gott!

Here am I, sweating, sick, and hot,
And there the shadowed waters fresh
Lean up to embrace the naked flesh.
Temperamentvoll German Jews
Drink beer around; – and *there* the dews
Are soft beneath a morn of gold.
Here tulips bloom as they are told;
Unkempt about those hedges blows
An English unofficial rose;
And there the unregulated sun

Slopes down to rest when day is done,
And wakes a vague unpunctual star,
A slippered Hesper; and there are
Meads towards Haslingfield and Coton
Where *das Betreten*'s not *verboten.*

εἴθε γενοίμην . . . would I were
In Grantchester, in Grantchester! –
Some, it may be, can get in touch
With Nature there, or Earth, or such.
And clever modern men have seen
A Faun a-peeping through the green,
And felt the Classics were not dead,
To glimpse a Naiad's reedy head,
Or hear the Goat-foot piping low: . . .
But these are things I do not know.
I only know that you may lie
Day-long and watch the Cambridge sky,
And, flower-lulled in sleepy grass,
Hear the cool lapse of hours pass,
Until the centuries blend and blur
In Grantchester, in Grantchester. . . .
Still in the dawnlit waters cool
His ghostly Lordship swims his pool,
And tries the strokes, essays the tricks,
Long learnt on Hellespont, or Styx.
Dan Chaucer hears his river still
Chatter beneath a phantom mill.
Tennyson notes, with studious eye,
How Cambridge waters hurry by . . .

And in that garden, black and white,
Creep whispers through the grass all night;
And spectral dance, before the dawn,
A hundred Vicars down the lawn;
Curates, long dust, will come and go
On lissom, clerical, printless toe;
And oft between the boughs is seen
The sly shade of a Rural Dean . . .
Till, at a shiver in the skies,
Vanishing with Satanic cries,
The prim ecclesiastic rout
Leaves but a startled sleeper-out,
Grey heavens, the first bird's drowsy calls,
The falling house that never falls.

God! I will pack, and take a train,
And get me to England once again!
For England's the one land, I know,
Where men with Splendid Hearts may go;
And Cambridgeshire, of all England,
The shire for Men who Understand;
And of *that* district I prefer
The lovely hamlet Grantchester.
For Cambridge people rarely smile,
Being urban, squat, and packed with guile;
And Royston men in the far South
Are black and fierce and strange of mouth;
At Over they fling oaths at one,
And worse than oaths at Trumpington,
And Ditton girls are mean and dirty,

And there's none in Harston under thirty,
And folks in Shelford and those parts
Have twisted lips and twisted hearts,
And Barton men make Cockney rhymes,
And Coton's full of nameless crimes,
And things are done you'd not believe
At Madingley, on Christmas Eve.
Strong men have run for miles and miles,
When one from Cherry Hinton smiles;

Strong men have blanched, and shot their wives,
Rather than send them to St Ives;
Strong men have cried like babes, bydam,
To hear what happened at Babraham.
But Grantchester! ah, Grantchester!
There's peace and holy quiet there,
Great clouds along pacific skies,
And men and women with straight eyes,
Lithe children lovelier than a dream,
A bosky wood, a slumbrous stream,
And little kindly winds that creep
Round twilight corners, half asleep.
In Grantchester their skins are white;
They bathe by day, they bathe by night;
The women there do all they ought;
The men observe the Rules of Thought.
They love the Good; they worship Truth;
They laugh uproariously in youth;
(And when they get to feeling old,
They up and shoot themselves, I'm told) . . .

Ah God! to see the branches stir
Across the moon at Grantchester!
To smell the thrilling-sweet and rotten
Unforgettable, unforgotten
River-smell, and hear the breeze
Sobbing in the little trees.
Say, do the elm-clumps greatly stand
Still guardians of that holy land?
The chestnuts shade, in reverend dream,
The yet unacademic stream?
Is dawn a secret shy and cold
Anadyomene, silver-gold?
And sunset still a golden sea
From Haslingfield to Madingley?
And after, ere the night is born,
Do hares come out about the corn?
Oh, is the water sweet and cool,
Gentle and brown, above the pool?
And laughs the immortal river still
Under the mill, under the mill?
Say, is there Beauty yet to find?
And Certainty? and Quiet kind?
Deep meadows yet, for to forget
The lies, and truths, and pain? . . . Oh! yet
Stands the Church clock at ten to three?
And is there honey still for tea?

Travel

'Twas when I was in Neu Strelitz
I broke my heart in little bits.

So while I sat in the Müritz train
I glued the bits together again.

But when I got to Amerhold,
I felt the glue would never hold.

And now that I'm home to Barton Hill,
I know once broken is broken still.

1912

In Freiburg Station

In Freiburg station, waiting for a train,
I saw a Bishop in puce gloves go by.
Now God may thunder furious from the sky,
Shattering all my glory into pain,
And joy turn stinking rotten, hope be vain,
Night fall on little laughters, little loves,
And better Bishops don more glorious gloves,
While I go down in darkness; what care I?

There is one memory God can never break,
There is one splendour more than all the pain,
There is one secret that shall never die,
Star-crowned I stand and sing, for that hour's sake.
In Freiburg station, waiting for a train,
I saw a Bishop with puce gloves go by.

1912

Fragment on Painters

There is an evil which that Race attaints
Who represent God's World with oily paints,
Who mock the Universe, so rare and sweet,
With spots of colour on a canvas sheet,
Defile the Lovely and insult the Good
By scrawling upon little bits of wood.
They'd snare the moon, and catch the immortal sun
With madder brown and pale vermilion,
Entrap an English evening's magic hush . . .

c.1912

Sometimes Even Now . . .

Sometimes even now I may
Steal a prisoner's holiday,
Slip, when all is worst, the bands,
   Hurry back, and duck beneath
Time's old tyrannous groping hands,
   Speed away with laughing breath
Back to all I'll never know,
Back to you, a year ago.

Truant there from Time and Pain,
What I had, I find again:
Sunlight in the boughs above,
   Sunlight in your hair and dress,
The Hands too proud for all but Love,
   The Lips of utter kindliness,
The Heart of bravery swift and clean
   Where the best was safe, I knew,
And laughter in the gold and green,
   And song, and friends, and ever you
With smiling and familiar eyes,
   You – but friendly: you – but true.

And Innocence accounted wise,
   And Faith the fool, the pitiable.
Love so rare, one would swear
   All of earth for ever well –

Careless lips and flying hair,
    And little things I may not tell.

It does but double the heart-ache
When I wake, when I wake.

c.1912

The Fish

In a cool curving world he lies
And ripples with dark ecstasies.
The kind luxurious lapse and steal
Shapes all his universe to feel
And know and be; the clinging stream
Closes his memory, glooms his dream,
Who lips the roots o' the shore, and glides
Superb on unreturning tides.
Those silent waters weave for him
A fluctuant mutable world and dim,
Where wavering masses bulge and gape
Mysterious, and shape to shape
Dies momently through whorl and hollow,
And form and line and solid follow
Solid and line and form to dream
Fantastic down the eternal stream;
An obscure world, a shifting world,
Bulbous, or pulled to thin, or curled,
Or serpentine, or driving arrows,
Or serene slidings, or March narrows.
There slipping wave and shore are one,
And weed and mud. No ray of sun,
But glow to glow fades down the deep
(As dream to unknown dream in sleep);
Shaken translucency illumes
The hyaline of drifting glooms;
The strange soft-handed depth subdues
Drowned colour there, but black to hues,
As death to living, decomposes –
Red darkness of the heart of roses,

Blue brilliant from dead starless skies,
And gold that lies behind the eyes,
The unknown unnameable sightless white
That is the essential flame of night,
Lustreless purple, hooded green,
The myriad hues that lie between
Darkness and darkness! . . .

                              And all's one
Gentle, embracing, quiet, dun,
The world he rests in, world he knows,
Perpetual curving. Only – grows
An eddy in that ordered falling,
A knowledge from the gloom, a calling
Weed in the wave, gleam in the mud –
The dark fire leaps along his blood;
Dateless and deathless, blind and still,
The intricate impulse works its will;
His woven world drops back; and he,
Sans providence, sans memory,
Unconscious and directly driven,
Fades to some dank sufficient heaven.

O world of lips, O world of laughter,
Where hope is fleet and thought flies after,
Of lights in the clear night, of cries
That drift along the wave and rise
Thin to the glittering stars above,
You know the hands, the eyes of love!
The strife of limbs, the sightless clinging

The infinite distance, and the singing
Blown by the wind, a flame of sound,
The gleam, the flowers, and vast around
The horizon, and the heights above –
You know the sigh, the song of love!

But there the night is close, and there
Darkness is cold and strange and bare;
And the secret deeps are whisperless;
And rhythm is all deliciousness;
And joy is in the throbbing tide,
Whose intricate fingers beat and glide
In felt bewildering harmonies
Of trembling touch; and music is
The exquisite knocking of the blood.
Space is no more, under the mud;
His bliss is older than the sun.
Silent and straight the waters run.
The lights, the cries, the willows dim,
And the dark tide are one with him.

Munich, March 1911

Mummia

As those of old drank mummia
   To fire their limbs of lead,
Making dead kings from Africa
   Stand pander to their bed;

Drunk on the dead, and medicined
   With spiced imperial dust,
In a short night they reeled to find
   Ten centuries of lust.

So I, from paint, stone, tale, and rhyme,
   Stuffed love's infinity,
And sucked all lovers of all time
   To rarefy ecstasy.

Helen's the hair shuts out from me
   Verona's livid skies;
Gypsy the lips I press; and see
   Two Antonys in your eyes.

The unheard invisible lovely dead
   Lie with us in this place,
And ghostly hands above my head
   Close face to straining face;

Their blood is wine along our limbs;
   Their whispering voices wreathe
Savage forgotten drowsy hymns
   Under the names we breathe;

Woven from their tomb, and one with it,
    The night wherein we press;
Their thousand pitchy pyres have lit
    Your flaming nakedness.

For the uttermost years have cried and clung
    To kiss your mouth to mine;
And hair long dust was caught, was flung,
    Hand shaken to hand divine,

And Life has fired, and Death not shaded,
    All Time's uncounted bliss,
And the height o' the world has flamed and faded, –
    Love, that our love be this!

1911

Dead Men's Love

There was a damned successful Poet;
   There was a Woman like the Sun.
And they were dead. They did not know it.
      They did not know their time was done.
            They did not know his hymns
            Were silence; and her limbs,
            That had served Love so well,
            Dust, and a filthy smell.

And so one day, as ever of old,
   Hands out, they hurried, knee to knee;
On fire to cling and kiss and hold
   And, in the other's eyes, to see
            Each his own tiny face,
            And in that long embrace
            Feel lip and breast grow warm
            To breast and lip and arm.

So knee to knee they sped again,
   And laugh to laugh they ran, I'm told,
Across the streets of Hell . . .
                  And then
      They suddenly felt the wind blow cold,
            And knew, so closely pressed,
            Chill air on lip and breast,
            And, with a sick surprise,
            The emptiness of eyes.

Munich, 27 February 1911

[67]

Colloquial

It was not that you said I thought you knew,
Or that you thought I said that you, my dear,
Felt what I felt you felt. If it were clear,
Had God given soul to me, or sense to you,
Or guts, indeed, to either of the two,
Had it been worth a smile, or worth a tear,
Heart of my heart.

February 1911

Thoughts on the Shape of the Human Body

How can we find? how can we rest? how can
We, being gods, win joy, or peace, being man?
We, the gaunt zanies of a witless Fate,
Who love the unloving, and the lover hate,
Forget the moment ere the moment slips,
Kiss with blind lips that seek beyond the lips,
Who want, and know not what we want, and cry
With crooked mouths for Heaven, and throw it by.
Love's for completeness! No perfection grows
'Twixt leg, and arm, elbow, and ear, and nose,
And joint, and socket; but unsatisfied
Sprawling desires, shapeless, perverse, denied.
Finger with finger wreathes; we love, and gape,
Fantastic shape to mazed fantastic shape,
Straggling, irregular, perplexed, embossed,
Grotesquely twined, extravagantly lost
By crescive paths and strange protuberant ways
From sanity and from wholeness and from grace.
How can love triumph, how can solace be,
Where fever turns toward fever, knee toward knee?
Could we but fill to harmony, and dwell
Simple as our thought and as perfectible,
Rise disentangled from humanity
Strange whole and new into simplicity,
Grow to a radiant round love, and bear
Unfluctuant passion for some perfect sphere,
Love moon to moon unquestioning, and be
Like the star Lunisequa, steadfastly
Following the round clear orb of her delight,
Patiently ever, through the eternal night!

c.1911

[69]

A Letter to a Live Poet

Sir, since the last Elizabethan died,
Or, rather, that more Paradisal muse,
Blind with much light, passed to the light more glorious
Or deeper blindness, no man's hand, as thine,
Has, on the world's most noblest chord of song,
Struck certain magic strains. Ears satiate
With the clamorous, timorous whisperings of to-day,
Thrilled to perceive once more the spacious voice
And serene utterance of old. We heard
– With rapturous breath half-held, as a dreamer dreams
Who dares not know it dreaming, lest he wake –
The odorous, amorous style of poetry,
The melancholy knocking of those lines,
The long, low soughing of pentameters,
– Or the sharp of rhyme as a bird's cry –
And the innumerable truant polysyllables
Multitudinously twittering like a bee.
Fulfilled our hearts were with that music then,
And all the evenings sighed it to the dawn,
And all the lovers heard it from all the trees.
All of the accents upon all the norms!
– And ah! the stress on the penultimate!
We never knew blank verse could have such feet.

Where is it now? Oh, more than ever, now
I sometimes think no poetry is read
Save where some sepultured Caesura bled,
Royally incarnadining all the line.
Is the imperial iamb laid to rest,
And the young trochee, having done enough?

Ah! turn again! Sing so to us, who are sick
Of seeming-simple rhymes, bizarre emotions,
Decked in the simple verses of the day,
Infinite meaning in a little gloom,
Irregular thoughts in stanzas regular,
Modern despair in antique metres, myths
Incomprehensible at evening,
And symbols that mean nothing in the dawn.
The slow lines swell. The new style sighs. The Celt
Moans round with many voices.
                                                God! to see
Gaunt anapaests stand up out of the verse,
Combative accents, stress where no stress should be,
Spondee on spondee, iamb on choriamb,
The thrill of all the tribrachs in the world,
And all the vowels rising to the E!
To hear the blessed mutter of those verbs,
Conjunctions passionate toward each other's arms,
And epithets like amaranthine lovers
Stretching luxuriously to the stars,
All prouder pronouns than the dawn, and all
The thunder of the trumpets of the noun!

January 1911

Sonnet Reversed

Hand trembling towards hand; the amazing lights
Of heart and eye. They stood on supreme heights.

Ah, the delirious weeks of honeymoon!
    Soon they returned, and, after strange adventures,
Settled at Balham by the end of June.
    Their money was in Can. Pacs. B. Debentures,
And in Antofagastas. Still he went
    Cityward daily; still she did abide
At home. And both were really quite content
    With work and social pleasures. Then they died.
They left three children (besides George, who drank):
    The eldest Jane, who married Mr Bell,
William, the head-clerk in the County Bank,
    And Henry, a stock-broker, doing well.

Lulworth, 1 January 1911

[72]

The Hill

Breathless, we flung us on the windy hill,
   Laughed in the sun, and kissed the lovely grass.
   You said, 'Through glory and ecstasy we pass;
Wind, sun, and earth remain, the birds sing still,
When we are old, are old. . . .' 'And when we die
   All's over that is ours; and life burns on
Through other lovers, other lips,' said I,
   'Heart of my heart, our heaven is now, is won!'

'We are Earth's best, that learnt her lesson here.
   Life is our cry. We have kept the faith!' we said;
   'We shall go down with unreluctant tread
Rose-crowned into the darkness!' . . . Proud we were,
And laughed, that had such brave true things to say.
– And then you suddenly cried, and turned away.

December 1910

[73]

Lines Written in the Belief that the Ancient Roman Festival of the Dead was called Ambarvalia

Swings the way still by hollow and hill,
    And all the world's a song;
  'She's far,' it sings me, 'but fair,' it rings me,
    'Quiet,' it laughs, 'and strong!'

Oh! spite of the miles and years between us,
    Spite of your chosen part,
I do remember; and I go
    With laughter in my heart.

So above the little folk that know not,
    Out of the white hill-town,
High up I clamber; and I remember;
    And watch the day go down.

Gold is my heart, and the world's golden,
    And one peak tipped with light;
And the air lies still about the hill
    With the first fear of night;

Till mystery down the soundless valley
    Thunders, and dark is here;
And the wind blows, and the light goes,
    And the night is full of fear.

And I know, one night, on some far height,
    In the tongue I never knew,
I yet shall hear the tidings clear
    From them that were friends of you.

They'll call the news from hill to hill,
   Dark and uncomforted,
Earth and sky and the winds; and I
   Shall know that you are dead.

I shall not hear your trentals,
   Nor eat your arval bread;
For the kin of you will surely do
   Their duty by the dead.

Their little dull greasy eyes will water;
   They'll paw you, and gulp afresh.
They'll sniffle and weep, and their thoughts
      will creep
   Like flies on the cold flesh.

They will put pence on your grey eyes,
   Bind up your fallen chin,
And lay you straight, the fools that loved you
   Because they were your kin.

They will praise all the bad about you,
   And hush the good away,
And wonder how they'll do without you,
   And then they'll go away.

But quieter than one sleeping,
   And stranger than of old,
You will not stir for weeping,
   You will not mind the cold;

But through the night the lips will laugh not,
    The hands will be in place,
And at length the hair be lying still
    About the quiet face.

With snuffle and sniff and handkerchief,
    And dim and decorous mirth,
With ham and sherry, they'll meet to bury
    The lordliest lass of earth.

The little dead hearts will tramp ungrieving
    Behind lone-riding you,
The heart so high, the heart so living,
    Heart that they never knew.

I shall not hear your trentals,
    Nor eat your arval bread,
Nor with smug breath tell lies of death
    To the unanswering dead.

With snuffle and sniff and handkerchief,
    The folk who loved you not
Will bury you, and go wondering
    Back home. And you will rot.

But laughing and half-way up to heaven,
    With wind and hill and star,
I yet shall keep, before I sleep,
    Your Ambarvalia.

1910

[76]

The Life Beyond

He wakes, who never thought to wake again,
  Who held the end was Death. He opens eyes
Slowly, to one long livid oozing plain
  Closed down by the strange eyeless heavens. He lies;
  And waits; and once in timeless sick surmise
Through the dead air heaves up an unknown hand,
Like a dry branch. No life is in that land,
  Himself not lives, but is a thing that cries;
An unmeaning point upon the mud; a speck
  Of moveless horror; an Immortal One
Cleansed of the world, sentient and dead; a fly
  Fast-stuck in grey sweat on a corpse's neck.

I thought when love for you died, I should die.
It's dead. Alone, most strangely, I live on.

April–September 1910

The Descent

Because you called, I left the mountain height,
Bleak nurse and neighbour to Infinity,
The sunlit solitude of Day, the high
Lone conversation with the lonely night;
These, and my fellows, I'd forgotten quite,
The stars and hills and silence and the wind,
And from my radiant uplands chose the blind
Nooks of your lost perpetual twilight.

For there your white and hungry hands were gleaming,
Your troublous mouth. And there we found desire
Asleep with sorrow, children lightly dreaming,
And laughter laid between close-lying faces.
There we found love in little hidden places,
Lost human love between the mist and mire.

c.1910

Flight

Voices out of the shade that cried,
   And long noon in the hot calm places,
And children's play by the wayside,
   And country eyes, and quiet faces –
   All these were round my steady paces.

Those that I could have loved went by me;
   Cool gardened homes slept in the sun;
I heard the whisper of water nigh me,
   Saw hands that beckoned, shone, were gone
   In the green and gold. And I went on.

For if my echoing footfall slept,
   Soon a far whispering there'd be
Of a little lonely wind that crept
   From tree to tree, and distantly
   Followed me, followed me. . . .

But the blue vaporous end of day
   Brought peace, and pursuit baffled quite,
Where between pine-woods dipped the way.
   I turned, slipped in and out of sight.
   I trod as quiet as the night.

The pine-boles kept perpetual hush;
   And in the boughs wind never swirled.
I found a flowering lowly bush,
   And bowed, slid in, and sighed and curled,
   Hidden at rest from all the world.

Safe! I was safe, and glad, I knew!
  Yet – with cold heart and cold wet brows
I lay. And the dark fell. . . . There grew
  Meward a sound of shaken boughs;
  And ceased, above my intricate house;

And silence, silence, silence found me. . . .
  I felt the unfaltering movement creep
Among the leaves. They shed around me
  Calm clouds of scent, that I did weep;
  And stroked my face. I fell asleep.

1910

The Goddess in the Wood

In a flowered dell the Lady Venus stood,
   Amazed with sorrow. Down the morning one
   Far golden horn in the gold of trees and sun
Rang out; and held; and died. . . . She thought the wood
Grew quieter. Wing, and leaf, and pool of light
   Forgot to dance. Dumb lay the unfailing stream;
   Life one eternal instant rose in dream
Clear out of time, poised on a golden height. . . .

Till a swift terror broke the abrupt hour.
The gold waves purled amidst the green above her;
   And a bird sang. With one sharp-taken breath,
By sunlit branches and unshaken flower,
The immortal limbs flashed to the human lover,
   And the immortal eyes to look on death.

March 1910

Dust

When the white flame in us is gone,
   And we that lost the world's delight
Stiffen in darkness, left alone
   To crumble in our separate night;

When your swift hair is quiet in death,
   And through the lips corruption thrust
Has stilled the labour of my breath –
   When we are dust, when we are dust! –

Not dead, not undesirous yet,
   Still sentient, still unsatisfied,
We'll ride the air, and shine, and flit,
   Around the places where we died,

And dance as dust before the sun,
   And light of foot, and unconfined,
Hurry from road to road, and run
   About the errands of the wind.

And every mote, on earth or air,
   Will speed and gleam, down later days,
And like a secret pilgrim fare
   By eager and invisible ways,

Nor ever rest, nor ever lie,
   Till, beyond thinking, out of view,
One mote of all the dust that's I
   Shall meet one atom that was you.

Then in some garden hushed from wind,
　　Warm in a sunset's afterglow,
The lovers in the flowers will find
　　A sweet and strange unquiet grow

Upon the peace; and, past desiring,
　　So high a beauty in the air,
And such a light, and such a quiring,
　　And such a radiant ecstasy there,

They'll know not if it's fire, or dew,
　　Or out of earth, or in the height,
Singing, or flame, or scent, or hue,
　　Or two that pass, in light, to light,

Out of the garden higher, higher. . . .
　　But in that instant they shall learn
The shattering ecstasy of our fire,
　　And the weak passionless hearts will burn

And faint in that amazing glow,
　　Until the darkness close above;
And they will know – poor fools, they'll know! –
　　One moment, what it is to love.

December 1909–March 1910

Desertion

So light we were, so right we were, so fair faith shone,
And the way was laid so certainly, that, when I'd gone,
What dumb thing looked up at you? Was it something
   heard,
Or a sudden cry, that meekly and without a word
You broke the faith, and strangely, weakly, slipped apart?
You gave in – you, the proud of heart, unbowed of heart!
Was this, friend, the end of all that we could do?
And have you found the best for you, the rest for you?
Did you learn so suddenly (and I not by!)
Some whispered story, that stole the glory from the sky,
And ended all the splendid dream, and made you go
So dully from the fight we know, the light we know?

O faithless! the faith remains, and I must pass
Gay down the way, and on alone. Under the grass
You wait; the breeze moves in the trees, and stirs, and calls,
And covers you with white petals, with light petals.
There it shall crumble, frail and fair, under the sun,
O little heart, your brittle heart; till day be done,
And the shadows gather, falling light, and, white with dew,
Whisper, and weep; and creep to you. Good sleep to you!

March 1910

[84]

Success

I think if you had loved me when I wanted;
  If I'd looked up one day, and seen your eyes,
And found my wild sick blasphemous prayer granted,
  And your brown face, that's full of pity and wise,
Flushed suddenly; the white godhead in new fear
  Intolerably so struggling, and so shamed;
Most holy and far, if you'd come all too near,
  If earth had seen Earth's lordliest wild limbs tamed,
Shaken, and trapped, and shivering, for *my* touch –
  Myself should I have slain? or that foul you?
But this the strange gods, who had given so much,
  To have seen and known you, this they might not do.
One last shame's spared me, one black word's un-spoken;
And I'm alone; and you have not awoken.

January 1910

[85]

Sonnet

I said I splendidly loved you; it's not true.
    Such long swift tides stir not a land-locked sea.
On gods or fools the high risk falls – on you –
    The clean clear bitter-sweet that's not for me.
Love soars from earth to ecstasies unwist.
    Love is flung Lucifer-like from Heaven to Hell.
But – there are wanderers in the middle mist,
    Who cry for shadows, clutch, and cannot tell
Whether they love at all, or, loving, whom:
    An old song's lady, a fool in fancy dress,
Or phantoms, or their own face on the gloom;
    For love of Love, or from heart's loneliness.
Pleasure's not theirs, nor pain. They doubt, and sigh
And do not love at all. Of these am I.

January 1910

[86]

The One Before the Last

I dreamt I was in love again
  With the One Before the Last,
And smiled to greet the pleasant pain
  Of that innocent young past.

But I jumped to feel how sharp had been
  The pain when it did live,
How the faded dreams of Nineteen-ten
  Were Hell in Nineteen-five.

The boy's woe was as keen and clear,
  The boy's love just as true,
And the One Before the Last, my dear,
  Hurt quite as much as you.

*   *   *

Sickly I pondered how the lover
  Wrongs the unanswering tomb,
And sentimentalizes over
  What earned a better doom.

Gently he tombs the poor dim last time,
  Strews pinkish dust above,
And sighs, 'The dear dead boyish pastime!
  But *this* – ah, God! – is Love!'

– Better oblivion hide dead true loves,
  Better the night enfold,

Than men, to eke the praise of new loves,
  Should lie about the old!

*　*　*

Oh! bitter thoughts I had in plenty.
  But here's the worst of it –
I shall forget, in Nineteen-twenty,
  You ever hurt a bit!

11 January 1910

Kindliness

When love has changed to kindliness –
Oh, love, our hungry lips, that press
So tight that Time's an old god's dream
Nodding in heaven, and whisper stuff
Seven million years were not enough
To think on after, make it seem
Less than the breath of children playing,
A blasphemy scarce worth the saying,
A sorry jest, 'When love has grown
To kindliness – to kindliness!' . . .
And yet – the best that either's known
Will change, and wither, and be less,
At last, than comfort, or its own
Remembrance. And when some caress
Tendered in habit (once a flame
All heaven sang out to) wakes the shame
Unworded, in the steady eyes
We'll have, – *that* day, what shall we do?
Being so noble, kill the two
Who've reached their second-best? Being wise,
Break cleanly off, and get away,
Follow down other windier skies
New lures, alone? Or shall we stay,
Since this is all we've known, content
In the lean twilight of such day,
And not remember, not lament?
That time when all is over, and
Hand never flinches, brushing hand;
And blood lies quiet, for all you're near;
And it's but spoken words we hear,

Where trumpets sang; when the mere skies
Are stranger and nobler than your eyes;
And flesh is flesh, was flame before;
And infinite hungers leap no more
In the chance swaying of your dress;
And love has changed to kindliness.

c.1910

Dining-Room Tea

When you were there, and you, and you,
Happiness crowned the night; I too,
Laughing and looking, one of all,
I watched the quivering lamplight fall
On plate and flowers and pouring tea
And cup and cloth; and they and we
Flung all the dancing moments by
With jest and glitter. Lip and eye
Flashed on the glory, shone and cried,
Improvident, unmemoried;
And fitfully and like a flame
The light of laughter went and came.
Proud in their careless transience moved
The changing faces that I loved.

Till suddenly, and otherwhence,
I looked upon your innocence.
For lifted clear and still and strange
From the dark woven flow of change
Under a vast and starless sky
I saw the immortal moment lie.
One instant I, an instant, knew
As God knows all. And it and you
I, above Time, oh, blind! could see
In witless immortality.
I saw the marble cup; the tea,
Hung on the air, an amber stream;
I saw the fire's unglittering gleam,
The painted flame, the frozen smoke.
No more the flooding lamplight broke

On flying eyes and lips and hair;
But lay, but slept unbroken there,
On stiller flesh, and body breathless,
And lips and laughter stayed and deathless,
And words on which no silence grew.
Light was more alive than you.
For suddenly, and otherwhence,
I looked on your magnificence.
I saw the stillness and the light,
And you, august, immortal, white,
Holy and strange; and every glint
Posture and jest and thought and tint
Freed from the mask of transiency,
Triumphant in eternity,
Immote, immortal.

               Dazed at length
Human eyes grew, mortal strength
Wearied; and Time began to creep.
Change closed about me like a sleep.
Light glinted on the eyes I loved.
The cup was filled. The bodies moved.
The drifting petal came to ground.
The laughter chimed its perfect round.
The broken syllable was ended.
And I, so certain and so friended,
How could I cloud, or how distress,
The heaven of your unconsciousness?
Or shake at Time's sufficient spell,
Stammering of lights unutterable?

The eternal holiness of you,
The timeless end, you never knew,
The peace that lay, the light that shone.
You never knew that I had gone
A million miles away, and stayed
A million years. The laughter played
Unbroken round me; and the jest
Flashed on. And we that knew the best
Down wonderful hours grew happier yet.
I sang at heart, and talked, and eat,
And lived from laugh to laugh, I too,
When you were there, and you, and you.

c.1910

A Channel Passage

The damned ship lurched and slithered. Quiet and quick
   My cold gorge rose; the long sea rolled; I knew
I must think hard of something, or be sick;
   And could think hard of only one thing – *you*!
You, you alone could hold my fancy ever!
   And with you memories come, sharp pain, and dole.
Now there's a choice – heartache or tortured liver!
   A sea-sick body, or a you-sick soul!

Do I forget you? Retchings twist and tie me,
   Old meat, good meals, brown gobbets, up I throw.
Do I remember? Acrid return and slimy,
   The sobs and slobber of a last year's woe.
And still the sick ship rolls. 'Tis hard, I tell ye,
To choose 'twixt love and nausea, heart and belly.

December 1909

Victory

All night the ways of Heaven were desolate,
    Long roads across a gleaming empty sky.
    Outcast and doomed and driven, you and I,
Alone, serene beyond all love or hate,
Terror or triumph, were content to wait,
    We, silent and all-knowing. Suddenly
    Swept through the heaven, low-crouching from on high,
One horseman, downward to the earth's low gate.

Oh, perfect from the ultimate height of living,
    Lightly we turned, through wet woods blossom-hung,
Into the open. Down the supernal roads,
    With plumes a-tossing, purple flags far-flung,
Rank upon rank, unbridled, unforgiving,
    Thundered the black battalions of the Gods.

June 1909

Day and Night

Through my heart's palace Thoughts unnumbered throng;
    And there, most quiet and, as a child, most wise,
High-throned you sit, and gracious. All day long
    Great Hopes gold-armoured, jester Fantasies,
    And pilgrim Dreams, and little beggar Sighs,
Bow to your benediction, go their way.
    And the grave jewelled courtier Memories
Worship and love and tend you, all the day.

But, when I sleep, and all my thoughts go straying,
    When the high session of the day is ended,
And darkness comes; then, with the waning light,
    By lilied maidens on your way attended,
Proud from the wonted throne, superbly swaying,
    You, like a queen, pass out into the night.

1909

The Charm

In darkness the loud sea makes moan;
And earth is shaken, and all evils creep
About her ways.
                    Oh, now to know you sleep!
Out of the whirling blinding moil, alone,
Out of the slow grim fight,
One thought to wing – to you, asleep,
In some cool room that's open to the night,
Lying half-forward, breathing quietly,
One white hand on the white
Unrumpled sheet, and the ever-moving hair
Quiet and still at length! . . .

Your magic and your beauty and your strength,
Like hills at noon or sunlight on a tree,
Sleeping prevail in earth and air.

In the sweet gloom above the brown and white
Night benedictions hover; and the winds of night
Move gently round the room, and watch you there,
And through the dreadful hours
The trees and waters and the hills have kept
The sacred vigil while you slept,
And lay a way of dew and flowers
Where your feet, your morning feet, shall tread.
And still the darkness ebbs about your bed.
Quiet, and strange, and loving-kind, you sleep.
And holy joy about the earth is shed;
And holiness upon the deep.

8 November 1909

Finding

From the candles and dumb shadows,
    And the house where love had died,
I stole to the vast moonlight
    And the whispering life outside.
But I found no lips of comfort,
    No home in the moon's light
(I, little and lone and frightened
    In the unfriendly night),
And no meaning in the voices. . . .
    Far over the lands, and through
The dark, beyond the ocean,
    I willed to think of *you*!
For I knew, had you been with me
    I'd have known the words of night,
Found peace of heart, gone gladly
    In comfort of that light.

Oh! the wind with soft beguiling
    Would have stolen my thought away;
And the night, subtly smiling,
    Came by the silver way;
And the moon came down and danced to me,
    And her robe was white and flying;
And trees bent their heads to me
    Mysteriously crying;
And dead voices wept around me;
    And dead soft fingers thrilled;
And the little gods whispered
                                But ever
    Desperately I willed;

Till all grew soft and far
   And silent . . .
              And suddenly
I found you white and radiant,
   Sleeping quietly,
Far out through the tides of darkness.
   And I there in that great light
Was alone no more, nor fearful;
   For there, in the homely night,
Was no thought else that mattered,
   And nothing else was true,
But the white fire of moonlight,
   And a white dream of you.

1909

Song

'Oh! Love,' they said, 'is King of Kings,
   And Triumph is his crown.
Earth fades in flame before his wings,
   And Sun and Moon bow down.' –
But that, I knew, would never do;
   And Heaven is all too high.
So whenever I meet a Queen, I said,
   I will not catch her eye.

'Oh! Love,' they said, and 'Love,' they said,
   'The gift of Love is this;
A crown of thorns about thy head,
   And vinegar to thy kiss!' –
But Tragedy is not for me;
   And I'm content to be gay.
So whenever I spied a Tragic Lady,
   I went another way.

And so I never feared to see
   You wander down the street,
Or come across the fields to me
   On ordinary feet.
For what they'd never told me of,
   And what I never knew,
It was that all the time, my love,
   Love would be merely you.

c.1909

Paralysis

For moveless limbs no pity I crave,
    That never were swift! Still all I prize,
Laughter and thought and friends, I have;
    No fool to heave luxurious sighs
For the woods and hills that I never knew.
The more excellent way's yet mine! And you

Flower-laden come to the clean white cell,
    And we talk as ever – am I not the same?
With our hearts we love, immutable,
    You without pity, I without shame.
We talk as of old; as of old you go
Out under the sky, and laughing, I know,

Flit throught the streets, your heart all me;
    Till you gain the world beyond the town.
Then – I fade from your heart, quietly;
    And your fleet steps quicken. The strong down
Smiles you welcome there; the woods that love you
Close lovely and conquering arms above you.

O ever-moving, O lithe and free!
    Fast in my linen prison I press
On impassable bars, or emptily
    Laugh in my great loneliness.

And still in the white neat bed I strive
Most impotently against that gyve;
Being less now than a thought, even,
To you alone with your hills and heaven.

July 1909

[101]

Town and Country

Here, where love's stuff is body, arm and side
  Are stabbing-sweet 'gainst chair and lamp and wall.
In every touch more intimate meanings hide;
  And flaming brains are the white heart of all.

Here, million pulses to one centre beat:
  Closed in by men's vast friendliness, alone,
Two can be drunk with solitude, and meet
  On the sheer point where sense with knowing's one.

Here the green-purple clanging royal night,
  And the straight lines and silent walls of town,
And roar, and glare, and dust, and myriad white
  Undying passers, pinnacle and crown

Intensest heavens between close-lying faces
  By the lamp's airless fierce ecstatic fire;
And we've found love in little hidden places,
  Under great shades, between the mist and mire.

Stay! though the woods are quiet, and you've heard
  Night creep along the hedges. Never go
Where tangled foliage shrouds the crying bird,
  And the remote winds sigh, and waters flow!

Lest – as our words fall dumb on windless noons,
  Or hearts grow hushed and solitary, beneath
Unheeding stars and unfamiliar moons,
  Or boughs bend over, close and quiet as death, –

Unconscious and unpassionate and still,
  Cloud-like we lean and stare as bright leaves stare,
And gradually along the stranger hill
  Our unwalled loves thin out on vacuous air,

And suddenly there's no meaning in our kiss,
  And your lit upward face grows, where we lie,
Lonelier and dreadfuller than sunlight is,
  And dumb and mad and eyeless like the sky.

c.1909

Menelaus and Helen

I

Hot through Troy's ruin Menelaus broke
   To Priam's palace, sword in hand, to sate
   On that adulterous whore a ten years' hate
And a king's honour. Through red death, and smoke,
And cries, and then by quieter ways he strode,
   Till the still innermost chamber fronted him.
   He swung his sword, and crashed into the dim
Luxurious bower, flaming like a god.

High sat white Helen, lonely and serene.
   He had not remembered that she was so fair,
And that her neck curved down in such a way;
And he felt tired. He flung the sword away,
   And kissed her feet, and knelt before her there,
The perfect Knight before the perfect Queen.

II

So far the poet. How should he behold
   That journey home, the long connubial years?
   He does not tell you how white Helen bears
Child on legitimate child, becomes a scold,
Haggard with virtue. Menelaus bold
   Waxed garrulous, and sacked a hundred Troys
   'Twixt noon and supper. And her golden voice
Got shrill as he grew deafer. And both were old.
Often he wonders why on earth he went
   Troyward, or why poor Paris ever came.

Oft she weeps, gummy-eyed and impotent;
    Her dry shanks twitch at Paris' mumbled name.
So Menelaus nagged; and Helen cried;
And Paris slept on by Scamander side.

1909

Lust

How should I know? The enormous wheels of will
   Drove me cold-eyed on tired and sleepless feet.
Night was void arms and you a phantom still,
   And day your far light swaying down the street.
As never fool for love, I starved for you;
   My throat was dry and my eyes hot to see.
Your mouth so lying was most heaven in view,
   And your remembered smell most agony.

Love wakens love! I felt your hot wrist shiver,
   And suddenly the mad victory I planned
     Flashed real, in your burning bending head. . . .
My conqueror's blood was cool as a deep river
   In shadow; and my heart beneath your hand
     Quieter than a dead man on a bed.

1909

Jealousy

When I see you, who were so wise and cool,
Gazing with silly sickness on that fool
You've given your love to, your adoring hands
Touch his so intimately that each understands,
I know, most hidden things; and when I know
Your holiest dreams yield to the stupid bow
Of his red lips, and that the empty grace
Of those strong legs and arms; that rosy face,
Has beaten your heart to such a flame of love,
That you have given him every touch and move,
Wrinkle and secret of you, all your life,
– Oh! then I know I'm waiting, lover-wife,
For the great time when love is at a close,
And all its fruit's to watch the thickening nose
And sweaty neck and dulling face and eye,
That are yours, and you, most surely, till you die!
Day after day you'll sit with him and note
The greasier tie, the dingy wrinkling coat;
As prettiness turns to pomp, and strength to fat,
And love, love, love to habit!
                                         And after that,
When all that's fine in man is at an end,
And you, that loved young life and clean, must tend
A foul sick fumbling dribbling body and old,
When his rare lips hang flabby and can't hold
Slobber, and you're enduring that worst thing,
Senility's queasy furtive love-making,
And searching those dear eyes for human meaning,
Propping the bald and helpless head, and cleaning
A scrap that life's flung by, and love's forgotten, –

Then you'll be tired; and passion dead and rotten;
And he'll be dirty, dirty!
                    O lithe and free
And lightfoot, that the poor heart cries to see,
That's how I'll see your man and you! –
                              But you
– Oh, when *that* time comes, you'll be dirty too!

1909

Blue Evening

My restless blood now lies a-quiver,
  Knowing that always, exquisitely,
This April twilight on the river
  Stirs anguish in the heart of me.

For the fast world in that rare glimmer
  Puts on the witchery of a dream,
The straight grey buildings, richly dimmer,
  The fiery windows, and the stream

With willows leaning quietly over,
  The still ecstatic fading skies . . .
And all these, like a waiting lover,
  Murmur and gleam, lift lustrous eyes,

Drift close to me, and sideways bending
  Whisper delicious words.
                    But I
Stretch terrible hands, uncomprehending,
  Shaken with love; and laugh; and cry.

My agony made the willows quiver;
  I heard the knocking of my heart
Die loudly down the windless river,
  I heard the pale skies fall apart,

And the shrill stars' unmeaning laughter,
  And my voice with the vocal trees
Weeping. And Hatred followed after,
  Shrilling madly down the breeze.

In peace from the wild heart of clamour,
    A flower in moonlight, she was there,
Was rippling down white ways of glamour
    Quietly laid on wave and air.

Her passing left no leaf a-quiver.
    Pale flowers wreathed her white, white brows.
Her feet were silence on the river;
    And 'Hush!' she said, between the boughs.

May 1909

The Voice

Safe in the magic of my woods
   I lay, and watched the dying light.
Faint in the pale high solitudes,
   And washed with rain and veiled by night,

Silver and blue and green were showing.
   And the dark woods grew darker still;
And birds were hushed; and peace was growing;
   And quietness crept up the hill;

And no wind was blowing . . .

And I knew
That this was the hour of knowing,
And the night and the woods and you
Were one together, and I should find
Soon in the silence the hidden key
Of all that had hurt and puzzled me –
Why you were you, and the night was kind,
And the woods were part of the heart of me.

And there I waited breathlessly,
Alone; and slowly the holy three,
The three that I loved, together grew
One, in the hour of knowing,
Night, and the woods, and you —

And suddenly
There was an uproar in my woods,
The noise of a fool in mock distress,
Crashing and laughing and blindly going,

Of ignorant feet and a swishing dress,
And a Voice profaning the solitudes.

The spell was broken, the key denied me,
And at length your flat clear voice beside me
Mouthed cheerful clear flat platitudes.

You came and quacked beside me in the wood.
You said, 'The view from here is very good!'
You said, 'It's nice to be alone a bit!'
And, 'How the days are drawing out!' you said.
You said, 'The sunset's pretty, isn't it?'

*   *   *

By God! I wish – I wish that you were dead!

April 1909

Sonnet

Oh! Death will find me, long before I tire
   Of watching you; and swing me suddenly
Into the shade and loneliness and mire
   Of the last land! There, waiting patiently,

One day, I think, I'll feel a cool wind blowing,
   See a slow light across the Stygian tide,
And hear the Dead about me stir, unknowing,
   And tremble. And *I* shall know that you have died,

And watch you, a broad-browed and smiling dream,
   Pass, light as ever, through the lightless host,
Quietly ponder, start, and sway, and gleam –
   Most individual and bewildering ghost! –

And turn, and toss your brown delightful head
Amusedly, among the ancient Dead.

April 1909

Choriambics

Ah! not now, when desire burns, and the wind calls,
    and the suns of spring
Light-foot dance in the woods, whisper of life, woo
    me to wayfaring:
Ah! not now should you come, now when the road
    beckons, and good friends call,
Where are songs to be sung, fights to be fought, yea!
    and the best of all,
Love, on myriad lips fairer than yours, kisses you
    could not give! . . .
Dearest, why should I mourn, whimper, and whine,
    I that have yet to live?
Sorrow will I forget, tears for the best, love on the
    lips of you,
Now, when dawn in the blood wakes, and the sun
    laughs up the eastern blue;
I'll forget and be glad!
        Only at length, dear, when the great day ends,
When love dies with the last light, and the last song
    has been sung, and friends
All are perished, and gloom strides on the heaven:
    then, as alone I lie,
'Mid Death's gathering winds, frightened and dumb,
    sick for the past, may I
Feel you suddenly there, cool at my brow; then may
    I hear the peace
Of your voice at the last, whispering love, calling, ere

all can cease
In the silence of death; then may I see dimly, and
    know, a space,
Bending over me, last light in the dark, once, as of old,
    your face.

December 1908

II

Here the flame that was ash, shrine that was void, lost
   in the haunted wood,
I have tended and loved, year upon year, I in the
   solitude
Waiting, quiet and glad-eyed in the dark, knowing
   that once a gleam
Glowed and went through the wood. Still I abode
   strong in a golden dream,
Unrecaptured.

                For I, I that had faith, knew that a face
                would glance
One day, white in the dim woods, and a voice call,
   and a radiance
Fill the grove, and the fire suddenly leap . . . and, in
   the heart of it,
End of labouring, you! Therefore I kept ready the
   altar, lit
The flame, burning apart.

              Face of my dreams vainly in vision white
Gleaming down to me, lo! hopeless I rise now. For
   about midnight
Whispers grew through the wood suddenly, strange
   cries in the boughs above
Grated, cries like a laugh. Silent and black then
   through the sacred grove
Great birds flew, as a dream, troubling the leaves,
   passing at length.

             I knew,
Long expected and long loved, that afar, God of the
   dim wood, you

Somewhere lay, as a child sleeping, a child suddenly
   reft from mirth.
White and wonderful yet, white in your youth,
   stretched upon foreign earth,
God, immortal and dead!
             Therefore I go; never to rest, or win
Peace, and worship of you more, and the dumb wood
   and the shrine therein.

December 1908

The Jolly Company

The stars, a jolly company,
    I envied, straying late and lonely;
And cried upon their revelry:
    'O white companionship! You only
In love, in faith unbroken dwell,
Friends radiant and inseparable!'

Light-heart and glad they seemed to me
    And merry comrades (*even so
God out of Heaven may laugh to see
    The happy crowds; and never know
That in his lone obscure distress
Each walketh in a wilderness*).

But I, remembering, pitied well
    And loved them, who, with lonely light,
In empty infinite spaces dwell,
    Disconsolate. For, all the night,
I heard the thin gnat-voices cry,
Star to faint star, across the sky.

November 1908

Sleeping Out: Full Moon

They sleep within. . . .
I cower to the earth, I waking, I only.
High and cold thou dreamest, O queen,
   high-dreaming and lonely.

We have slept too long, who can hardly win
The white one flame, and the night-long crying;
The viewless passers; the world's low sighing
With desire, with yearning,
To the fire unburning,
To the heatless fire, to the flameless ecstasy! . . .

Helpless I lie.
And around me the feet of thy watchers tread.
There is a rumour and a radiance of wings above my
   head,
An intolerable radiance of wings. . . .

All the earth grows fire,
White lips of desire
Brushing cool on the forehead, croon slumbrous
   things.
Earth fades; and the air is thrilled with ways,
Dewy paths full of comfort. And radiant bands,
The gracious presence of friendly hands,
Help the blind one, the glad one, who stumbles and
   strays,

Stretching wavering hands, up, up, through the praise
Of a myriad silver trumpets, through cries,

To all glory, to all gladness, to the infinite height,
To the gracious, the unmoving, the mother eyes,
And the laughter, and the lips, of light.

August 1908

Day That I Have Loved

Tenderly, day that I have loved, I close your eyes,
  And smooth your quiet brow, and fold your thin
    dead hands.
The grey veils of the half-light deepen; colour dies.
  I bear you, a light burden, to the shrouded sands,

Where lies your waiting boat, by wreaths of the sea's
    making
  Mist-garlanded, with all grey weeds of the water
    crowned.
  There you'll be laid, past fear of sleep or hope of
    waking;
  And over the unmoving sea, without a sound,

Faint hands will row you outward, out beyond our sight,
  Us with stretched arms and empty eyes on the far-
    gleaming
And marble sand . . .
            Beyond the shifting cold twilight,
  Further than laughter goes, or tears, further than
    dreaming,

There'll be no port, no dawn-lit islands! But the drear
  Waste darkening, and, at length, flame ultimate on
    the deep.
Oh, the last fire – and you, unkissed, unfriended there!
  Oh, the lone way's red ending, and we not there to weep!

(We found you pale and quiet, and strangely crowned
    with flowers,

Lovely and secret as a child. You came with us,
Came happily, hand in hand with the young dancing hours,
   High on the downs at dawn!) Void now and tenebrous,

The grey sands curve before me. . . .
                    From the inland meadows,
   Fragrant of June and clover, floats the dark, and fills
The hollow sea's dead face with little creeping shadows,
   And the white silence brims the hollow of the hills.

Close in the nest is folded every weary wing,
   Hushed all the joyful voices; and we, who held you dear,
Eastward we turn and homeward, alone,
      remembering . . .
   Day that I loved, day that I loved, the Night is here!

1908

Second Best

Here in the dark, O heart;
Alone with the enduring Earth, and Night,
And Silence, and the warm strange smell of clover;
Clear-visioned, though it break you; far apart
From the dead best, the dear and old delight;
Throw down your dreams of immortality,
O faithful, O foolish lover!
Here's peace for you, and surety; here the one
Wisdom – the truth! – 'All day the good glad sun
Showers love and labour on you, wine and song;
The greenwood laughs, the wind blows, all day long
Till night.' And night ends all things.
                                                      Then shall be
No lamp relumed in heaven, no voices crying,
Or changing lights, or dreams and forms that hover!
(And, heart, for all your sighing,
That gladness and those tears are over, over. . . .)

And has the truth brought no new hope at all,
Heart, that you're weeping yet for Paradise?
Do they still whisper, the old weary cries?
'*'Mid youth and song, feasting and carnival,*
Through laughter, through the roses, as of old
Comes Death, on shadowy and relentless feet,
Death, unappeasable by prayer or gold;
Death is the end, the end!'
Proud, then, clear-eyed and laughing, go to greet
Death as a friend!

Exile of immortality, strongly wise,
Strain through the dark with undesirous eyes
To what may lie beyond it. Sets your star,
O heart, for ever! Yet, behind the night,
Waits for the great unborn, somewhere afar,
Some white tremendous daybreak. And the light,
Returning, shall give back the golden hours,
Ocean a windless level, Earth a lawn
Spacious and full of sunlit dancing-places,
And laughter, and music, and, among the flowers,
The gay child-hearts of men, and the child-faces,
O heart, in the great dawn!

1908

Pine-Trees and the Sky: Evening

I'd watched the sorrow of the evening sky,
And smelt the sea, and earth, and the warm clover,
And heard the waves, and the seagull's mocking cry.

And in them all was only the old cry,
That song they always sing – 'The best is over!
You may remember now, and think, and sigh,
O silly lover!'
And I was tired and sick that all was over,
And because I,
For all my thinking, never could recover
One moment of the good hours that were over.
And I was sorry and sick, and wished to die.

Then from the sad west turning wearily,
I saw the pines against the white north sky,
Very beautiful, and still, and bending over
Their sharp black heads against a quiet sky.
And there was peace in them; and I
Was happy, and forgot to play the lover,
And laughed, and did no longer wish to die;
Being glad of you, O pine-trees and the sky!

Lulworth, 8 July 1907

Failure

Because God put His adamantine fate
   Between my sullen heart and its desire,
I swore that I would burst the Iron Gate,
   Rise up, and curse Him on His throne of fire.
Earth shuddered at my crown of blasphemy,
   But Love was as a flame about my feet;
   Proud up the Golden Stair I strode; and beat
Thrice on the Gate, and entered with a cry –

All the great courts were quiet in the sun,
   And full of vacant echoes: moss had grown
Over the glassy pavement, and begun
   To creep within the dusty council-halls.
An idle wind blew round an empty throne
   And stirred the heavy curtains on the walls.

1908

The Song of the Pilgrims

Halted around the fire by night, after moon-set,
they sing this beneath the trees

What light of unremembered skies
Hast thou relumed within our eyes,
Thou whom we seek, whom we shall find? . . .
A certain odour on the wind,
Thy hidden face beyond the west,
These things have called us; on a quest
Older than any road we trod,
More endless than desire. . . .

      Far God,

Sigh with thy cruel voice, that fills
The soul with longing for dim hills
And faint horizons! For there come
Grey moments of the antient dumb
Sickness of travel, when no song
Can cheer us; but the way seems long;
And one remembers. . . .

      Ah! the beat

Of weary unreturning feet,
And songs of pilgrims unreturning! . . .
The fires we left are always burning
On the old shrines of home. Our kin
Have built them temples, and therein
Pray to the Gods we know; and dwell
In little houses lovable,
Being happy (we remember how!)
And peaceful even to death. . . .

      O Thou,

God of all long desirous roaming,

Our hearts are sick of fruitless homing,
And crying after lost desire.
Hearten us onward! as with fire
Consuming dreams of other bliss.
The best Thou givest, giving this
Sufficient thing – to travel still
Over the plain, beyond the hill,
Unhesitating through the shade,
Amid the silence unafraid,
Till, at some sudden turn, one sees
Against the black and muttering trees
Thine altar, wonderfully white,
Among the Forests of the Night.

March 1908

On the Death of Smet-Smet,
the Hippopotamus Goddess

Song of a tribe of the ancient Egyptians

(*The Priests within the Temple*)
She was wrinkled and huge and hideous? She was our
    Mother.
She was lustful and lewd? – but a God; we had none other.
In the day She was hidden and dumb, but at nightfall
    moaned in the shade;
We shuddered and gave Her Her will in the darkness;
    we were afraid.

(*The People without*)
> *She sent us pain,*
>   *And we bowed before Her;*
> *She smiled again*
>   *And bade us adore Her.*
> *She solaced our woe*
>   *And soothed our sighing;*
> *And what shall we do*
>   *Now God is dying?*

(*The Priests within*)
She was hungry and ate our children; – how should
    we stay Her?
She took our young men and our maidens; – ours to
    obey Her.
We were loathèd and mocked and reviled of all
    nations; that was our pride.

She fed us, protected us, loved us, and killed us; now
    She has died.

(*The People without*)
                She was so strong;
                    But Death is stronger.
                She ruled us long;
                    But Time is longer.
                She solaced our woe
                    And soothed our sighing;
                And what shall we do
                    Now God is dying?

1908

Seaside

Swiftly out from the friendly lilt of the band,
    The crowd's good laughter, the loved eyes of men,
    I am drawn nightward; I must turn again
Where, down beyond the low untrodden strand,
There curves and glimmers outward to the unknown
    The old unquiet ocean. All the shade
Is rife with magic and movement. I stray alone
    Here on the edge of silence, half afraid,

Waiting a sign. In the deep heart of me
The sullen waters swell towards the moon,
And all my tides set seaward.
              From inland
Leaps a gay fragment of some mocking tune,
That tinkles and laughs and fades along the sand,
And dies between the seawall and the sea.

1908

Wagner

Creeps in half wanton, half asleep,
  One with a fat wide hairless face.
He likes love-music that is cheap;
  Likes women in a crowded place;
    And wants to hear the noise they're making.

His heavy eyelids droop half-over,
  Great pouches swing beneath his eyes.
He listens, thinks himself the lover,
  Heaves from his stomach wheezy sighs;
    He likes to feel his heart's a-breaking.

The music swells. His gross legs quiver.
  His little lips are bright with slime.
The music swells. The women shiver.
  And all the while, in perfect time,
    His pendulous stomach hangs a-shaking.

Queen's Hall, 1908

In Examination

Lo! from quiet skies
In through the window my Lord the Sun!
And my eyes
Were dazzled and drunk with the misty gold,
The golden glory that drowned and crowned me
Eddied and swayed through the room . . .

                                    Around me,

To left and to right,
Hunched figures and old,
Dull blear-eyed scribbling fools, grew fair,
Ringed round and haloed with holy light.
Flame lit on their hair,
And their burning eyes grew young and wise,
Each as a God, or King of kings,
White-robed and bright
(Still scribbling all);
And a full tumultuous murmur of wings
Grew through the hall;
And I knew the white undying Fire,
And, through open portals,
Gyre on gyre,
Archangels and angels, adoring, bowing,
And a Face unshaded. . . .
Till the light faded;
And they were but fools again, fools unknowing,
Still scribbling, blear-eyed and stolid immortals.

February 1908

Sonnet: in time of Revolt

The thing must End. I am no boy! I AM
   NO BOY!! being twenty-one. Uncle, you make
   A great mistake, a very great mistake,
In chiding me for letting slip a 'Damn!'
What's more, you called me 'Mother's one ewe lamb,'
   Bade me 'refrain from swearing – for *her* sake –
   Till I'm grown up' . . . – By God! I think you take
Too much upon you, Uncle William!

You say I am your brother's only son.
I know it. And, 'What of it?' I reply.
My heart's resolvéd. *Something must be done.*
So shall I curb, so baffle, so suppress
This too avuncular officiousness,
Intolerable consanguinity.

January 1908

Song of the Children in Heaven

In evil places far away
And naughty times for ever gone
We were so good, the Angels say,
That now God lets us sit upon
The golden floor of glassy stone.

He is so good and kind, and yet
(Don't tell Him) the great floor of glass
Is rather hard. We can't forget
The bad old world. We wish it was
Just warm, sweet-smelling, tumbly grass.

And when on whistles and toy drums
We make a loud amusing noise,
Some large official seraph comes
And scolds, and takes away our toys,
Bids us sit still and be good boys.

And when a baby laughs up here
Or rolls his crown about in play,
There is a pause. God looks severe;
The Angels frown, and sigh and pray,
And some-one takes the crown away.

August 1907

The Little Dog's Day

All in the town were still asleep,
When the sun came up with a shout and a leap.
In the lonely streets unseen by man,
A little dog danced. And the day began.

All his life he'd been good, as far as he could,
And the poor little beast had done all that he should.
But this morning he swore, by Odin and Thor
And the Canine Valhalla – he'd stand it no more!
So his prayer he got granted – to do just what he
    wanted,
Prevented by none, for the space of one day.
'Jam incipiebo,[1] *sedere facebo,'*[2]
In dog-Latin he quoth, *'Euge! sophos! hurray!'*

He fought with the he-dogs, and winked at the she-dogs,
A thing that had never been *heard* of before.
'For the stigma of gluttony, I care not a button!' he
Cried, and ate all he could swallow – and more.

He took sinewy lumps from the shins of old frumps,
And mangled the errand-boys – when he could get 'em.
He shammed furious *rabies,*[3] and bit all the babies,[3]
And followed the cats up the trees, and then ate 'em!
They thought 'twas the devil was holding a revel,
And sent for the parson to drive him away;

[1] Now we're off.

[2] I'll make them sit up.

[3] Pronounce either to suit rhyme.

For the town never knew such a hullaballoo
As that little dog raised – till the end of that day.

> *When the blood-red sun had gone burning down,*
> *And the lights were lit in the little town,*
> *Outside, in the gloom of the twilight grey,*
> *The little dog died when he'd had his day.*

July 1907

The Wayfarers

Is it the hour? We leave this resting-place
   Made fair by one another for a while.
Now, for a god-speed, one last mad embrace;
   The long road then, unlit by your faint smile.
Ah! the long road! and you so far away!
Oh, I'll remember! but . . . each crawling day
   Will pale a little your scarlet lips, each mile
Dull the dear pain of your remembered face.

. . . Do you think there's a far border town,
     somewhere,
   The desert's edge, last of the lands we know,
     Some gaunt eventual limit of our light,
   In which I'll find you waiting; and we'll go
Together, hand in hand again, out there,
     Into the waste we know not, into the night?

June 1907

My Song

They are unworthy, these sad whining moods.
　　Shall I not make of Love some glorious thing? –
A song – and shout it through the dripping woods,
　　Till all the woods shall burgeon into Spring?
Because I've a mad longing for your eyes,
　　And once our eager lips met wonderfully,
Men shall find new delight in morning skies,
　　And all the stars will dance more merrily.

Yes, in the wonder of the last day-break,
God's Mother, on the threshold of His house,
　　Shall welcome in your white and perfect soul,
Kissing your brown hair softly for my sake;
　　And God's own hand will lay, as aureole,
My song, a flame of scarlet, on your brows.

June 1907

Ante Aram

Before thy shrine I kneel, an unknown worshipper,
  Chanting strange hymns to thee and sorrowful
    litanies,
Incense of dirges, prayers that are as holy myrrh.

Ah! goddess, on thy throne of tears and faint low sighs,
  Weary at last to theeward come the feet that err,
And empty hearts grown tired of the world's vanities.

How fair this cool deep silence to a wanderer
  Deaf with the roar of winds along the open skies!
Sweet, after sting and bitter kiss of sea-water,

The pale Lethean wine within thy chalices! . . .
  I come before thee, I, too tired wanderer
To heed the horror of the shrine, the distant cries,

And evil whispers in the gloom, or the swift whirr
  Of terrible wings – I, least of all thy votaries,
With a faint hope to see the scented darkness stir,

And, parting, frame within its quiet mysteries
  One face, with lips than autumn-lilies tenderer,
And voice more sweet than the far plaint of viols is,

  Or the soft moan of any grey-eyed lute-player.

June 1907

Dawn

From the train between Bologna and Milan, second class

Opposite me two Germans snore and sweat.
  Through sullen swirling gloom we jolt and roar.
We have been here for ever: even yet
  A dim watch tells two hours, two aeons, more.
The windows are tight-shut and slimy-wet
  With a night's fœtor. There are two hours more;
Two hours to dawn and Milan; two hours yet.
  Opposite me two Germans sweat and snore. . . .

One of them wakes, and spits, and sleeps again.
  The darkness shivers. A wan light through the rain
Strikes on our faces, drawn and white. Somewhere
  A new day sprawls; and, inside, the foul air
Is chill, and damp, and fouler than before. . . .
  Opposite me two Germans sweat and snore.

1907

Song

Oh! that apple bloom, and the pale spring sun
And the cottage door;
I'll see them all, before I've done,
A many Aprils more.

And you, for all your fairy feet,
And your strange brown ways,
Won't wholly for ever by wood or street
Avoid one owlish gaze.

But – suddenly you, in white and blue,
By the cottage door,
And the blue and white of April weather,
And the apple-bloom – just these together
I'll see no more, no more.

c.1907

The Call

Out of the nothingness of sleep,
  The slow dreams of Eternity,
There was a thunder on the deep:
  I came, because you called to me.

I broke the Night's primeval bars,
  I dared the old abysmal curse,
And flashed through ranks of frightened stars
  Suddenly on the universe!

The eternal silences were broken;
  Hell became Heaven as I passed. –
What shall I give you as a token,
  A sign that we have met, at last?

I'll break and forge the stars anew,
  Shatter the heavens with a song;
Immortal in my love for you,
  Because I love you, very strong.

Your mouth shall mock the old and wise,
  Your laugh shall fill the world with flame,
I'll write upon the shrinking skies
  The scarlet splendour of your name,

Till Heaven cracks, and Hell thereunder
  Dies in her ultimate mad fire,
And darkness falls, with scornful thunder,
  On dreams of men and men's desire.

Then only in the empty spaces,
   Death, walking very silently,
Shall fear the glory of our faces
   Through all the dark infinity.

So, clothed about with perfect love,
   The eternal end shall find us one,
Alone above the Night, above
   The dust of the dead gods, alone.

February 1907

The Beginning

Some day I shall rise and leave my friends
And seek you again through the world's far ends,
You whom I found so fair,
(Touch of your hands and smell of your hair!),
My only god in the days that were.
My eager feet shall find you again,
Though the sullen years and the mark of pain
Have changed you wholly; for I shall know
(How could I forget having loved you so?),
In the sad half-light of evening,
The face that was all my sunrising.
So then at the ends of the earth I'll stand
And hold you fiercely by either hand,
And seeing your age and ashen hair
I'll curse the thing that once you were,
Because it is changed and pale and old
(Lips that were scarlet, hair that was gold!),
And I loved you before you were old and wise,
When the flame of youth was strong in your eyes,
– And my heart is sick with memories.

January 1907

The Vision of the Archangels

Slowly up silent peaks, the white edge of the world,
　Trod four archangels, clear against the unheeding sky,
Bearing, with quiet even steps, and great wings furled,
　A little dingy coffin; where a child must lie,
It was so tiny. (Yet, you had fancied, God could never
　Have bidden a child turn from the spring and the
　　sunlight,
And shut him in that lonely shell, to drop for ever
　Into the emptiness and silence, into the night. . . .)

They then from the sheer summit cast, and watched it fall,
　Through unknown glooms, that frail black coffin –
　　and therein
　God's little pitiful Body lying, worn and thin,
And curled up like some crumpled, lonely flower-petal –
Till it was no more visible; then turned again
With sorrowful quiet faces downward to the plain.

December 1906

The Song of the Beasts

Sung, on one night, in the cities, in the darkness

Come away! Come away!
Ye are sober and dull through the common day,
But now it is night!
It is shameful night, and God is asleep!
(Have you not felt the quick fires that creep
Through the hungry flesh, and the lust of delight,
And hot secrets of dreams that day cannot say?). . . .
. . . The house is dumb;
The night calls out to you. . . . Come, ah, come!
Down the dim stairs, through the creaking door,
Naked, crawling on hands and feet
– It is meet! it is meet!
Ye are men no longer, but less and more,
Beast and God. . . . Down the lampless street,
By little black ways, and secret places,
In darkness and mire,
Faint laughter around, and evil faces
By the star-glint seen – ah! follow with us!
For the darkness whispers a blind desire,
And the fingers of night are amorous. . . .
Keep close as we speed,
Though mad whispers woo you, and hot hands cling,
And the touch and the smell of bare flesh sting,
Soft flank by your flank, and side brushing side –
Tonight never heed!
Unswerving and silent follow with me,
Till the city ends sheer,
And the crook'd lanes open wide,
Out of the voices of night,

Beyond lust and fear,
To the level waters of moonlight,
To the level waters, quiet and clear,
To the black unresting plains of the calling sea.

1906

Vanitas

Laugh now and live! Our blood is young, our hearts
    are high.
Fragrant of life, aflame with roses, all the Spring
Thrills in our windy souls and woos to wayfaring;
And the glad sun goes laughing up the eastern sky.

Laugh now and live! the gods are with us. Death and tears
Are dreams we know not. Life, mysterious, divine,
Lifts to our scarlet mouths her young immortal wine,
And wreaths with roses all our passionate laughing years.

Only, – remember! The day passeth; not for long
Stays the mad joyance of our golden revelry.
The young eyes darken; the rose petals fade and die;
Sleep ends and crowns our carnival, silence our song.

Too soon the pale hour calls us! Suddenly cold and chill
Dies on our lips the jest, the joy within our heart:
From the loved comrades, the warm feast, we steal apart,
The lonely night before us. Pitifully still

Lie the young limbs, the feet that delicately trod
Life's fluting measures, the red lips that sang, the whole
White beauty of our body: and the startled soul
Flutters and fails before the darkness that is God.

March 1906

The Lost Lilies

'What if one heaven by sin be forfeited?'
    (Thus in my wilful bitterness I spake)
'More loves remain, though one young love be dead:
    Shall all my life be void, for a dream's sake?
    – Let me arise! Beauty yet waits, I wis,
    Red blooms more passionate than these wan lilies!'

So, after desolate questing through the years,
    At length I won to this dim languorous place,
Fragrant with night and roses. All my tears
    Fade from me, bending to hide my weary face
    Deep in this drowsy gloom of fragrances,
    And drown remembrance of my lost lilies.

Ah! surely here at length oblivion
    Shall crown my wandering, and this dim perfume
Cover away remembrance of things gone,
    In scented groves and passionate warm gloom!
    Surely more sweet the roses' purple kiss,
    Than the pale sorrow of my lost lilies!

Yet sometimes, in a still twilight, it may be,
    Even these roses scentless grow and stale;
Joy for a time seems but Satiety;
    The warm spells of the subtle darkness fail;
    Till the sick heart's memorial litanies
    Sigh for the pure grace of my lost lilies.

And all the murmur and scent of sun-setting
     Awake the passionate old dreams; and I
Sit weary-eyed in silent sorrowing,
     And nurse the old regrets that will not die,
   Remembering where the perfect beauty is,
   The immortal pallor of my lost lilies.

Autumn 1905

The Bastille

I

Sullen athwart the freedom of the skies
It frowned, and mocked the sun's high pageantry,
– Dawn of the cloudy hair and pleading eyes,
And the green sunset-light, –
With the dark threat of its immensity,
And sinister portent of all-shrouding night.
Round it the dead innumerable days
Clung, and the wraiths of years and seasons past,
– Spring, dancing young-eyed down the woodland ways;
Summer, the fragrant queen of long delight,
Languid with roses; Autumn, old and wan,
Wearily creeping graveward; and at last
Winter's oblivion.
So, while the silent feet of Time sped on,
It loomed tremendous, hateful in men's eyes,
Tyranny's presence. For in fear firm-set
Stood all the towers; of sorrow-laden gloom
The walls were built, and fluttering pale sighs;
And, darkening every life-enfolding tomb,
Passion and wild regret
And all captivity's unavailing cries.

II

There, through the grey monotony of years,
The grim walls held their secret; none might tell
Who drank therein the tainted cup of tears,
Blinded with memories intolerable,
Bereft of hopes and fears.

For them no passionate Spring-tide, as of yore,
Regal with hue and scent,
Flashed through the startled woods; nor, ere night fell,
Blossomed the budding West to rose of flame,
And robed the plains in purple; and no more
Fair Dawn was tremulous in the Orient.
But, in the darkening cell,
Silent, upon pale feet, the shadows came;
And the wan twilight died; and there was night.
Then on the darkness to the sleepless eyes
Glimmered sad memories,
Old dreams of love, old heavens forfeited,
Poignant as those dear visions of our light
That mock the shadowy unforgetful Dead.
Night-long with bitter heart each dreamt his dream;
One, how the fire-light gleam
Played redly on a loved face far away;
Another, it may be,
Of the seething wave, the shrill-exulting gale,
And irresistible thunder of the sea.

*　*　*

Till the gloom quivered, and the black grew pale,
And lo! the dawn was grey.

III

Never to them comes Death as to the free,
– The swift unbearable horror, and the night

That shrouds the horror; no stern mystery,
Veiled in the old impenetrable gloom,
Quenches their faltering light.
Nor theirs the fear those revellers know, to whom
Sudden across Life's clamorous laughing rout
The clear inexorable voices call,
Bidding them from this luminous festival
To the dim Unknown without.
Not so look these toward our Lady Death,
But as a well-loved friend in gentle wise
She seeks them; for her cool hand comforteth,
And in the shadowy purple of her eyes
Dwells quiet healing, as an even-tide
That soothes with sleepy breath
The odorous murmur of some garden-side
Till all the roses slumber. To the brain
Sick with the gloom and silence and old pain,
Calm-eyed and thrice-desired she comes, to bring –
Balm for the wound, rest for each weary thing,
To every prisoner the Great Release,
Death after life, joy after sorrowing,
And, after striving, peace.

IV

Huge over Paris, grey and motionless,
Its shadow brooded, while, swift year on year,
Faded four centuries;
Beneath that old immutable loneliness
Men swarmed and toiled, and all their dreary cries

Moaned up unheeded; vast and unseen a Fear
Gloomed like a darkness over every heart,
And chilled their inarticulate murmurings.
Only the gay Court, revelling apart,
From poverty far, and all grey-tinted things,
Wanton, and fair, and gay,
Sported like moths on glittering careless wings
Among life's fragrant buds and moon-kissed flowers,
Nor feared the slow inevitable day.
But, through the sunless hours,
France, as a sleeper, dumb, unheeding, lay;
Till a swift thunder thrilled the heavy air,
The purple gloom grew pallid; and at length
She from her slumber stirred, and woke to greet
Liberty, young and fair,
– Fair as a god triumphant in his strength,
Shades of the night still clinging about his feet,
But the glory of the sunrise on his hair.

v

Strong as great waters in autumnal flood,
Wave after wave insurgent, everywhence,
New-armed in Freedom's high magnificence,
The people gathered. To the red hearts aflame
All the pale streets cried wantonly for blood,
And all the resonant heavens clanged one name,
'To the Bastille!' and lo! –
Clamour of many feet on paven ways,
And voices distant-thundering, that grow,

[155]

And mount, and ring sonorous as the sea,
To break in a frenzy round the keep's dumb face,
The tower's funereal immobility.
Ever more near the tossing myriad sways;
The fire-ring narrows slowly; gate by gate,
Wall after wall, escarpment, bastion,
Bow to the tide that sweeps triumphant on,
Ravenous, hoarse, dark-menacing as Fate . . .
– Till a great cry goes crashing heavenward,
And the Bastille is won!
Then through the sun-forsaken drowsy air
Welcome the night, beneficent, dreamy-starred,
No hand may rest till stone be torn from stone,
Each infamy laid bare,
And tyranny's ancient stronghold overthrown.
Freedom is gained! The exultant paeans rise,
Noise of great ruining, and a sudden glare,
As fire victorious storms the trembling skies.

VI

How the bright glory of that early faith
Is faded now, and tarnished. For we know
Not by one sudden blow
Are peace and freedom won; nay, even yet
Grey poverty, and Sin that poisoneth,
Eat out men's hearts, and tyrannous Wealth is strong,
And almost we forget
Because the night of sorrowing is long.
Weary and faint we climb; still the road seems

Bitter with gloom and sorrow; still we grope,
Blind in the utter night; yet dimly gleams
The star of an infinite tremendous hope
That there shall come an ending, that at last,
Somewhere beyond our dreams,
The eternal day, the ultimate goal shall be,
All mystery revealed, the old made new;
Where, the quest over, sin and bondage past,
Men shall be Gods, and every vision true,
And Time Eternity.

1905

The Dawn

When on my night of life the Dawn shall break
   Scatt'ring the mist of dreams, the old sad gloom,
   Before that terrible sunrise of the tomb: –
Shall I forget the dull memorial ache?
Shall not my tired heart as a child awake
   Filling the dawn with music? nor retain
   Aught of the sad notes of my former strain,
But through that splendid dayspring rise and make
Beauty more beautiful, the dawn more fair?
   Only – I fear me that I may not find
That brave smile that once lit my sunless air,
   The bright swift eyes with purity there behind,
Nor see the pale cloud of her tossing hair
   Laugh and leap out along the desolate wind.

1905

August

Weary of summer heat,
    And sated of delight,
Glides the moon out, to meet,
    The hot kiss of the night,
    With listless feet.

Roses in every bed
    Strew fragrant leaves, and weep;
Towards each drooping head
    The stealthy shadows creep;
    Summer is dead.

One poppy sorroweth,
    Late-blown and desolate,
Bowed by the faint wind's breath,
    Knowing these twain await,
    Autumn and Death.

The thirsty flowers complain,
    Whimpering, half-afraid,
Till the dew soothes them again,
    And a God's voice through the shade
    Sighs, as in pain.

1905

Sorrow

I whispered to my sorrow, 'Come! Let us go hence
Far through the dusk, we two, to some dim shadowy place,
And there until the Night come, terrible, immense,
Muse only on her long-shut eyes and fragrant face: –
The day is long. Prithee, pale sorrow, let us hence!

Ah! let us go! the World's loud crying wearies me,
The pain and striving; surely the Gods will give me this,
To dream, and in memory's dim glass again to see
Her sorrowing mouth, and flesh more fair than pale lilies,
The beauty that I lost: – come, Sorrow, come with me!'

But with soft cruel words to me my Sorrow spake:
'Nay: for thy scorned deserted Gods will not relent.
Surely their pitiless immutable law shall break
Thine heart, too greatly loving, with slow punishment.'
Too tired for words I listened while my Sorrow spake.

'Labour and woe shall fill thy days, and Memory
Haunt all thy bitter paths, and make thy labour vain,
Tainting thine every brief delight; ah! not for thee
The gradual peace of solitude. Only remain
Toil without hope, and weariness, and memory.'

1905

Evening

Lo, now, the splendour of sun-setting!
  And the little fields are dim with mist.
Dewy and merciful through the shadows,
  Robed in purple and amethyst,
          Comes the hour of forgetting.

Not as the glory of day found us,
  In the dreams and folly of youth's delight:
But only the silent sleep remaineth
  Now, and the infinite starless night
          Lies coldly around us.

Nothing of passion or pale sorrow
  Moveth us there; we shall sleep apart
Lonely, unheeding; no sad memorial
  Yesterdays now shall touch our heart,
          Nor ever a morrow,

Rest for sick bodies and hearts aching!
    We shall sleep very soundly, you and I,
Sleep unbroken by passionate dreaming,
    Silence unmarred by sob or sigh,
          And – God guard us from waking!

1905

Man

Time drew towards its ending: every where,
Bent with their little sorrows and old pain,
Men cried to God. I heard the sound of it
Go mourning heavenward as a smoke, and there
Fall blindly before the pitiless Infinite
And cold un-heeding faces of the stars.

*   *   *

'Why are our hearts so full of questionings,
Of search, and passionate dreams, and vain desire?
Can we not live as other Life, content
With the few grey years we know, and asking not
Whence we have come and whither shall depart?
Why are we vexed with yearning? Surely it is
Enough for us to crouch about the fire
And laugh the irretrievable hours away,
Heedless of what may wait us in the gloom,
The muttering night beyond? Yet though we strive
So to live in the present and forget,
Ever the voice returning wakes again
The old insatiate yearning in our hearts,
Whispering words incomprehensible,
Infinity, Eternity, and – God.
Ah, we are tired: yet – it may be that now
Our age-long toiling draweth to its close.
For the earth is waxing old and full of sleep,
Being weary of the sins that men have wrought,
And heavy with their tears. Ever she nods
Brooding upon the springs of long ago,

Dreaming sick dreams; and wrapt in a grey mist
Slips tottering down into the silent night.
Therefore we think 'tis time that God took pity,
E'en as He said, and brought the eternal End,
Flinging the earth into the sun's white fires,
Tearing aside the worn robe of the heavens,
Quenching the light, and stamping the stars to dust,
And bringing back the terrible night that was.'

March 1905

In January

What shall I tell thee of?
Of the new sad memories one name can move?
Of the Heaven that Love brings? or of the Hell
That followed such Love?
Of these shall I tell?

I have not forgotten yet
The mist that shrouded all things, cold and wet;
The dripping bough: the sad smell of the rotten
Leaves. How should I forget?
Hast *thou* forgotten?

Dost thou remember now
How our eyes met; and all things changed; and how
A glorious light thrilled all that dim December,
And a bird sang on the bough?
Dost thou remember?

1905

The Return

Long had I dwelt in dreams and loneliness,
    Until thy sad voice sighed through the dusk to me,
    Hinting of joy, of better things to be,
Laughter and light beyond my dim distress.
Then I arose. Amid the fevered press
    Of hot-eyed men, across the desolate sea,
    Hoping a dreamer's hope, I sought for thee.
Wisdom at last I found, and weariness.

Nay, I was foolish, weak. I shall return,
    Back to the Night and Silence that I love,
    Back to my dreams. It may be even yet
The old fires on the old grey altars burn,
    The old Gods throng their shadowy haunted grove,
    Where I can sleep, and rest me, and – forget.

1905

The Pyramids

Where on Egyptian sand the lone sun fades
Hotly, and in the purple distance dies,
Near the eternal Nile old Memphis lies
Forgotten, and those three lone aeon-scarr'd
Monuments, keeping immemorial ward,
Dream of departed splendour and the shades
Of old Regalities.
Thus have they stood and seen the centuries
Flit by them like a dream,
And heard the roll and clangour of the years,
Bearing on men and their little hopes and fears
To the last peace of quiet Lethe stream.
Thus will they stand, and watch the mad world sway
Pulsing in endless haste,
Till the red dawn of that last day
When Earth shall vanish and the pale-starr'd waste
Of Heav'n, as a robe out-worn, be cast away.

II

The slaves who laboured, heaping stone on stone,
Whole-hewn from the live rock; the men who gazed
On these vast sepulchres of rock, slow-raised,
And went in a great wonder to their own
Far countries; yea, the Kings themselves for whom
These Pyramids were builded as a tomb
When they should leave that mighty Throne
And lay aside their Kingship with their breath; –
All hath the flood of Time caught up and thrown

Swift from this light into the dim Unknown,
The gloom that men call Death.
But here the waves of Time swell up and rage
Vainly: men die and nations wane,
Great Empires fall, change seizes all those things
Men hold immortal; yet do these remain,
Immutable, voiceless, lonely in their age,
Grey with the dust that once was kings.

III

How many nations have they seen arise,
And widen into greatness, and at length,
Tho' fair and firmly set to all men's eyes,
Yet sappèd from within
By luxury or sin,
Fall swiftly from the glory of their strength,
Humbled in far-spread ruin with the lies
That subtly wrought their downfall: first their own
Fair Egypt, old in Empire grown
Even when they were built: and afterwards
Innumerable ancient suzerainties,
– Syria and rock-walled Babylon,
And the wild uplands of the Indian bards,
China with her great sleeping millions, all
Sunk to mere names and faded memories.
So, too, the Western Empires, one by one,
Have fallen: Athens, great-hearted as the sea,
Behind whose guardian walls Greek liberty
Found refuge and a home,

Till windy words o'erwhelmèd her; and She
Whose sword had held the world in thrall,
Till all her heart was eaten by luxury,
That poison that so sweetly kills,
Proud in the girdle of her Seven Hills,
Indomitable Rome.

IV

So wind the nations in long pageant by,
Over a pathway paven with the dead,
Foul-stain'd and purple with the blood that's shed
In the vain merciless mad race
For dreams of 'Empire' and 'Supremacy'.
And mingling in the throng is seen the face
Of many a one who gazèd in his day
On these same monuments, and went his way,
Cheer'd by the calm that reft him for a space
Out of this clanging world of strife,
This grey despondency,
And let him see with visionary eye
Out and beyond our squalid Town of Life
The dim expanses of Eternity.
Egypt's forgotten rulers here are seen
Khufu, and Khafra, and Queen Sesostris,
Ramses the warrior, and that sad name
Of the Roman spouse of Egypt's last fair Queen,
To whom his Love was more than life or shame,
Who bartered all his Empire for a kiss.
Yet they have look'd on one of larger fame

[168]

Even than those puissant warriors the great
Child of the new-grown France, the Corsican
Whose more than human will had conquered Man,
And well-nigh conquered Fate.

V

Near to the Southward, even more old than they,
Lies the great Sphinx, half-buried in the sand,
Batter'd and scarr'd, the gaze of those who stay
But for a moment, and then hasten on
And do not understand.
Yet lies it, builded by an unknown hand
On some forgotten day,
And so shall lie, when we and ours are gone
Out of all history, vanished quite away
Into the long rest of Oblivion,
Still gazing eastward, waiting for the light,
Out and apart from the World's heat and strife,
Voiceless, inscrutable, and grey,
Type of that Riddle, old as the primal night,
The Riddle of our Life.

VI

Ah! when we muse upon the weight of years
That cover these grey tombs, how petty seem
The little things we dream,
The tissue of our loves and hopes and fears
That wraps us round and stifles us, till we

Hear not the slow chords of the rolling spheres,
The Eternal Music that God makes, nor see
How on the shadow of the night appears
The pale Dawn of the glory that shall be.

1904

The Path of Dreams

Go, heart, and pluck beside the Path of Dreams,
Where moans the wind along the shadowy streams,
   Sad garlands wreathed of the red mournful Roses,
      And lilies o' moon beams.

Strange blossoms faint upon that odorous air,
Vision, and wistful Memory; and there
   Love twofold with the purple bloom of Triumph
      And the wan leaf of Despair.

Go heart; go quickly; pluck and weave thereof
Dim garlands, scattering pallid dew above,
   And far across the sighing tides of darkness
      Lay them beside my Love.

c.1904

Afterwards

O brother, dost thou know what this thing means,
    to dread
  The cold inevitable dawn, the sickly light,
  The hours long passing, and the bells that toll and smite
Madness and swift blind pangs within the aching head?
Knowest thou this too, brother, when the day is fled
  How to the sleepless eyes the strange fears of the night
  Come mocking, and the bitter thoughts of old delight
Mix with the unforgiving faces of the Dead?

Ah, if thou know'st this sorrow, thou art even as I;
  As one who has long outlived his joy, and would forget;
  Who nurses in his festered soul a slave's dull hate
For this interminable hell of Life; and yet
  Shrinketh from ending it, in fear of what may wait
Behind the pitiless Silence of Eternity.

c.1904

Dedication

When I have laid my head upon the breast
Of kindly Earth, and infinite night above
Weighs heavy on mine eyes, and brings me rest
From all my sins and sorrows, and my love,

Then it may be that thou, O heart's desire,
Wilt chance upon these broken rhymes, that I
Fashioned and forged in the fierce hidden fire
Of this my love, the love wherein I die.

Will not a sudden gleam to thee make plain
In one great moment what thou hadst not seen?
Wilt thou not weep for great love given in vain,
And sigh to think of all that might have been?

c.1904

The Earth

Our Mother the Earth is weary; overhead
   Blaze the great torches of the planets seven,
   The moon mist-laden rides the eastern heaven,
Westward the Sun hath left the horizon red.
These are immortal; from the earth is fled
   The first clean rapture of her primal life.
   She is sore grievèd; laden with men's strife,
Woe of the living – burden of the dead.

Our Mother the Earth is weary; through the night
   I heard her laboured breathing, deep with pain;
   And thus the moaning swelled toward the sky;
'Let me not see anew the cold grey light,
   Merciful God – nor feel the dawn again',
   And still there came no answer to the cry.

1904

To them that Dream

O Brothers, we are Comrades on the way,
    We dreamers, we who have given our hearts to gain
    Some glorious Hope, and wake to find it vain.
Heed not the shame, the bitter things men say
In wrath and hatred; Though your souls be grey
    And all your lives a failure, yet take heart;
    Remember, we have chosen the better part;
Leave them in darkness, ours to seek the day.

Onward, though Faith grown tired has died, and Hope
    Breathed out her pitiful life beneath the rod
    Of wan Despair, – though Love's last golden spark
Flickered and ceased; we feebly, dimly grope,
    Seeking a light to lead us through the dark,
    Seeking the Unknown, stretching unto God.

1904

It Is Well

Nay, love, I weep not, but laugh o'er my dead,
My dreams long perished; though I forfeited
To save thee sorrow, joy unutterable –
I would not have it otherwise; 'twas well.

Well is it that I bear thy load of sin,
And fall defeated so *thou* mayest win;
And cast my heart before thee in the mire
To help thee upward to *thy* heart's desire.

And, when our Death dawns pale, and we must go,
Though infinite space may part us, this I know;
If, looking upward through the bars of Hell,
I see that face in Heaven, it will be well.

1903

God Give

God give that through the labour of my day
In dust and sweat,
These things may fade, and I forget
One curved mouth, and sad eyes far away,
One dream I dare not say –
And yet –
Ah yet, if it could be
That as the long day drew to evening,
And the light
Drooped like a weary lily o'er the sea,
Sudden across my sorrowing,
Healing and fragrant, with the fragrant night,
Thou should'st come back to me!
And I should see thy delicate feet returning,
The tremulous eyelids of my old delight,
The red lips yearning,
And all the beauty and supple youth of thee!
Ah! even thus, before my lonely rest
To feel on my lips thy lips' perfection pressed
Make sweet my ultimate sad breath;
Only to know
Thy cool voice murmuring low
Ere all be lost in silences of death,
And, as the last light fadeth from the skies,
The glamour of thine eyes.

1903

FRAGMENTS
WRITTEN DURING THE VOYAGE TO GALLIPOLI
APRIL 1915

Lines for an Ode-Threnody on England

All things are written in the mind.
There the sure hills have station; and the wind
Blows   in that placeless air.
And there the white and golden birds go flying;
And the stars wheel and shine; and woods are fair;
The light upon the snow is there;
                    and in that nowhere move
The trees and hands and waters that we love.

And she for whom we die, she the undying
Mother of men
England!

In Avons of the heart her rivers run.

She is with all we have loved and found and known,
Closed in the little nowhere of the brain.
Only, of all our dreams,
Not the poor heap of . . . dust and stone,
This local earth, set in terrestrial streams,
Not this man, giving all for gold,
Nor that who has found evil good, nor these
Blind millions, bought and sold . . .

She is not here, or now –
She is here, and now, yet nowhere –
We gave her birth, who bore us –
Our wandering feet have sought, but never found her –
She is built a long way off –
She, though all men be traitors, not betrayed –

Whose soil is love, and her stars justice, she –
Gracious with flowers,
And robed . . . and glorious in the sea.

She was in his eyes, but he could not see her,
And he was England, but he knew her not.

Other Fragments

They say Achilles in the darkness stirred,
And . . . Hector, his old enemy,
Moved the great shades that were his limbs.
    They heard
More than Olympian thunder on the sea.

                    Death and Sleep
        Bear many a young Sarpedon home.

And Priam and his fifty sons
Wake all amazed, and hear the guns,
   And shake for Troy again.

*　*　*

     'When Nobby tried', the stokers say,
       'To stop a shrapnel with his belly
     He   away,
       He left a lump of bleeding jelly'.
     But *he* went out, did Nobby Clark
     Upon the illimitable dark,
     Out of the fields where soldiers stray,
       Beyond parades, beyond reveille.

*　*　*

The poor scrap of a song that some man tried
 Down in the troop-decks forrard, brought again
 The day you sang it first, on a hill-side,
With April in the wind and in the brain.

And the woods were gold; and youth was
    in our hands.

*   *   *

                    Oh lovers parted,
Oh all you lonely over all the world,
You that look out at morning empty-hearted,
Or you, all night turning uncomforted.

Would God, would God, you could be comforted.

                    Eyes that weep,
And a long time for love; and, after, sleep.

*   *   *

And daylight, like a dust, sinks through the air,
And drifting, golds the ground . . .
                    A lark,
A voice in heaven, in fading deeps of light,
Drops, at length, home.

A wind of night, shy as the young hare
That steals even now out of the corn to play,
Stirs the pale river once, and creeps away.

*   *   *

The feet that ran with mine have found
    their goal,
The eyes that met my eyes have looked on night.
The firm limbs are no more; gone back to earth,
Easily mingling . . .
                      What is he yet,
Not living, lives, hath place in a few minds . . .
                           He wears
The ungathered blossom of quiet; stiller he
Than a deep well at noon, or lovers met;
Than sleep, or the heart after wrath. He is
The silence following great words of peace.

Index of Titles

Index of First Lines